CONTENTS

Welcome to
LEARNING TARGETS

Learning Targets is a series of practical teacher's resource books written to help you to plan and deliver well-structured, professional lessons in line with all the relevant curriculum documents.

Each Learning Target book provides exceptionally clear lesson plans that cover the whole of its stated curriculum plus a large bank of carefully structured copymasters. Links to the key curriculum documents are provided throughout to enable you to plan effectively.

The Learning Targets series have been written in response to the challenge confronting teachers not just to come up with teaching ideas which cover the curriculum but to ensure that they deliver high quality lessons every lesson with the emphasis on raising standards of pupil achievement.

The recent thinking from OFSTED, and the National Literacy and Numeracy Strategies on the key factors in effective teaching has been built into the structure of Learning Targets. These might briefly be summarised as follows:

➤➤ that effective teaching is active teaching directed to very clear objectives

➤➤ that good lessons are delivered with pace, rigour and purpose

➤➤ that good teaching requires a range of strategies - including interactive whole class sessions

➤➤ that ongoing formative assessment is essential to plan children's learning

➤➤ that differentiation is necessary but that it must be realistic.

The emphasis in Learning Targets is on absolute clarity. We have written and designed the books to enable you to access and deliver effective lessons as easily as possible, with the following aims:

➤➤ to plan and deliver rigorous, well-structured lessons

➤➤ to set explicit targets for achievement in every lesson that you teach

➤➤ to make the children aware of what they are going to learn

➤➤ to put the emphasis on direct, active teaching every time

➤➤ to make effective use of time and resources

➤➤ to employ the full range of recommended strategies: whole-class, group and individual work

➤➤ to differentiate for ability groups realistically

➤➤ to use ongoing formative assessment to plan your next step

➤➤ to have ready access to usable pupil copymasters to support your teaching.

The page opposite provides an at-a-glance guide to the key features of the Learning Targets lessons and explains how they will enable you deliver effective lessons.
The key to symbols on the lesson plans is set out here. ➤➤

How to deliver structured lessons with pace, rigour and purpose

Explicit targets for achievement in every lesson

Concise advice on preparation

Crystal clear lesson plan layouts

The full range of teaching strategies

Rigorous and practical activities

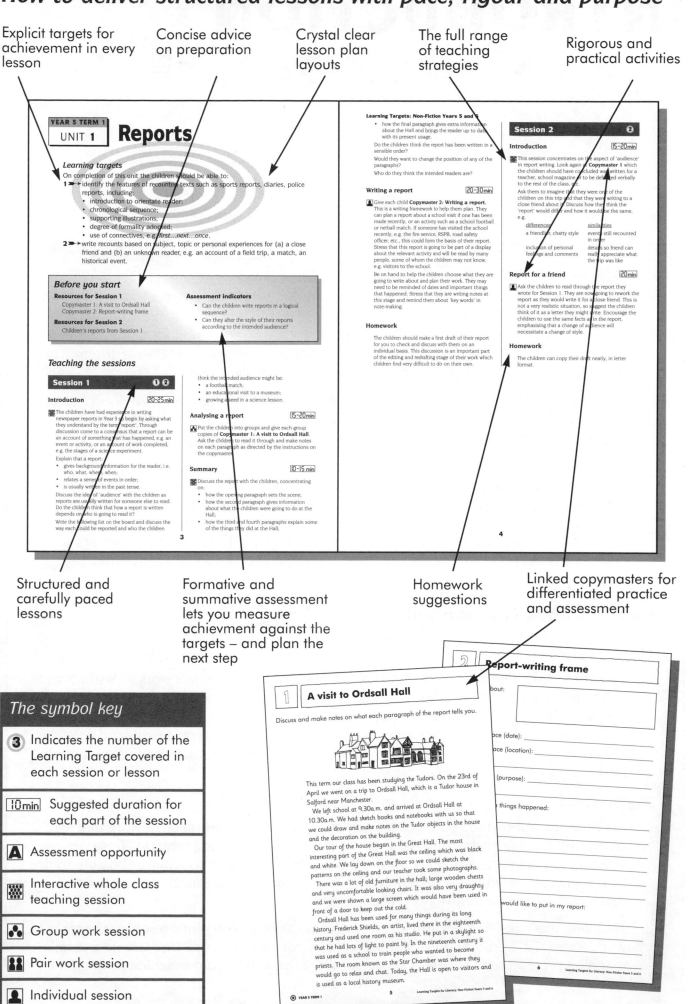

Structured and carefully paced lessons

Formative and summative assessment lets you measure achievment against the targets – and plan the next step

Homework suggestions

Linked copymasters for differentiated practice and assessment

The symbol key

(3)	Indicates the number of the Learning Target covered in each session or lesson
10min	Suggested duration for each part of the session
A	Assessment opportunity
	Interactive whole class teaching session
	Group work session
	Pair work session
	Individual session

INTRODUCTION

Learning Targets for Literacy: Non-Fiction *Years 5 and* 6 provides detailed coverage of comprehension and composition level work for English for non-fiction. Together with the accompanying book *Fiction and Poetry Years 5 and* 6, it provides an invaluable resource for text level work for the National Literacy Strategy and for Scotland P6–P7. The two other Learning Targets books at Key Stage 2, *Grammar and Punctuation* and *Spelling*, cover sentence and word level work respectively.

This book covers reading and writing non-fiction at the level of the text: how to read, understand and write all the relevant genres at Years 5 and 6. All the related decoding, spelling, handwriting and grammar skills for Key Stage 2 are covered in the other two books at this level.

This book is not, of course, a complete literacy scheme. It cannot provide you with all the resources needed to deliver text level literacy for non-fiction to your class. It is, however, a highly comprehensive resource book that covers all the main requirements through a series of well structured, detailed and specific lesson plans backed by linked copymasters that provide you with the pupil sheets you need to deliver the lessons.

How this book is organised.

The sections

The book is divided into six sections. Each one covers one term's work in Years 5 and 6 for the National Literacy Strategy and closely follows the range of work and the detailed plans for non-fiction on pages 44–55 of the National Literacy Strategy document. Each section begins with a short overview of the term's work and provides assessment objectives linked to copymasters. A National Literacy Strategy planner is also included at this point.

The units

Sections are subdivided into units. Each unit is an integrated piece of work that combines reading and writing skills to meet particular learning targets. These learning targets state explicitly what the children should aim to know or be able to do by the end of the unit and provide you with a set of clear, assessable objectives to teach any lesson on non-fiction at text level.

Together, the units in a section form an overall set of lesson plans to cover the term's work. They are 'free-standing' so that you can, for example, use Unit 2 from a term's teaching programme to meet a particular objective within your teaching programme without having undertaken Unit 1. In general, units at the beginning of a section are easier and difficulty builds up incrementally to a mastery of the assessment objectives outlined at the start. Children's progress can be summatively assessed using the assessment copymasters at the end of the section.

The sessions

Units are composed of a number of teaching 'sessions'. These teaching suggestions are very specific and detailed, and use the full range of teaching strategies required during the literacy hour: teacher-directed whole class, individual, pair and group work. Approximate times are suggested to enable you to fit the sessions into your literacy hour programme. In practice, of course, the times actually required will vary according to the children's ability and the way the sessions are going. You will find a key to the symbols used in the sessions on page v.

Within a unit, the sessions tend to increase in complexity. Particular sessions *may* be used independently of the overall unit for a particular purpose but the sessions within a unit are closely linked, being designed to provide a complete teaching programme that combines reading and writing non-fiction with best practice in teaching literacy skills. You will probably want to teach the sessions within the context of their whole units.

The copymasters

Photocopiable sheets can be found at the end of every unit and these are integral to teaching the sessions. As well as providing activities and information, they also include assessment sheets. Although a book of this kind cannot provide all the reading materials required to deliver the Strategy, it should not be necessary to seek out many extra resources to deliver the targeted literacy objectives. All the copymasters are reinforced by structured lesson plans.

Using this book alongside the National Literacy Strategy and the Scottish Guidelines

You will find a National Literacy Strategy planner for each term's work after the section introduction. This details the term's work and shows where you can find units and sessions to resource it. You will find that the learning targets closely follow the content and wording of the non-fiction requirements for Years 5 and 6 in the National Literacy Strategy document.

Each unit of work can supply the material for a string of literacy hours. Units can be broken up into their constituent sessions across the week, using the timings as an approximate guide. Many of the activities and sessions can be used very flexibly and differentiation within the sessions is as much by outcome as by activity. Every teacher will, of course, interpret the demands of the literacy hour individually in the light of their own situation.

Despite its Literacy Strategy structure, all the ideas in the book are equally applicable to the Scottish situation: they are, in essence, structured and effective ideas for good practice in literacy teaching in all situations. You will find an outline planner linking the book to the Scottish English Language 5–14 Guidelines on the next page.

Throughout Learning Targets, we have made a practice of mapping the contents of each book against the English Language 5–14 guidelines by attainment target. However, as the attainment targets for reading and writing that relate to non-fiction are rather general, we have here reproduced the programmes of study. Aspects of the programmes of study below are broadly covered in this book. Specific items are related to units of the book by year, term and unit: 5.1.1 indicates coverage in Year 5, Term 1, Unit 1.

READING

Reading for information

Level C: At this stage pupils will be helped to identify the sequence of information in short texts: 5.1.1
The teacher will continue to support pupils in questioning the nature of text and how information is likely to be organised: 5.1.1, 5.1.2
Pupils will be helped to experiment with ways of recording information: 5.1.1, 5.1.3

Level D: Pupils, in groups or individually, will be given practical reading tasks (e.g. using timetables, brochures, running a book club): 5.1.2
It is at this stage that other reference sources, (e.g. telephone directories), should be examined for their ways of ordering information: 5.2.2
It will be important for the pupils to decide, in advance of reading, the main aspects of the subject about which they want information: 5.1.3
Teachers should help pupils to see the value of varied formats for gathering and presenting information: flow charts, matrices, databases, notes, diagrams, illustrations, etc. 5.2.1

Level E: Pupils will encounter practical situations across the curriculum which will require them to read, understand and select relevant information in order to solve problems or carry out tasks of some complexity: 6.2.1
For a piece of personal research pupils will be helped: to establish a purpose; to develop appropriate presentation; to identify a variety of resources; and to use highlighting, underlining and other textual markers in identifying relevant information: 6.1.1, 6.1.3

Awareness of genre

Level C: In non-fiction texts, including newspapers, pupils will be helped to adjust reading approaches to the different ways information is presented: as aspects of a subject; as ideas supported by evidence; as events in chronological order; as facts built towards a conclusion: 5.1.1, 5.1.2, 5.3.2, 6.1.2, 6.2.1

Level D: With informational texts, teachers can now help pupils to recognise how texts dealing with different types of knowledge differ: how an account of a battle differs from a description of the life cycle of a butterfly, or from an argument for attending to dental health: 6.1.1
Practice in sequencing and prediction with such texts will lead pupils to familiarity with their various structures: 5.1.1

Level E: With non-fictional texts, teachers will help pupils to identify the ways in which the text presents its knowledge.

For example, a history text is very different from instructions on how to conduct an experiment in science. Pupils should look for evidence in the text of the purposes for which it was made: 6.2.2, 6.3.1

Knowledge about language

Level D: Fact and opinion are used to discuss the validity of an argument, the weighing of evidence and the identification of intentional or unintentional bias: 5.3.1, 5.3.2, 5.3.3, 6.1.1, 6.1.2
Layout, bold and italic type will be used in examining how the presentation of text can influence meaning and the ways that readers react: 5.3.1, 5.3.3, 6.2.2

Level E: Genre will now be regularly used as a description of categories of texts.
… discussion which centres on individual words, their origins, meanings and functions within texts: 5.2.1, 5.3.2

WRITING

Functional writing

Level C: Non-narrative writing is often undertaken in the context of other curricular areas such as environmental studies. The purpose and audience for writing of this nature should be clearly established: 5.1.1, 5.3.3
The teacher will help pupils make notes on, for example, a visit or a radio or TV programme and to build reports from these notes: 5.1.3, 5.2.1
Reports based on pupils' reading will involve the teacher in helping them to analyse the text and identify important data: 5.1.3, 5.2.1

Level D: Reading and discussing texts with their teacher and other pupils to identify the main forms associated with functional writing, pupils will be encouraged to produce a variety of different kinds of writing and to write succinctly: 5.2.1, 5.3.2, 6.1.3, 6.2.1, 6.3.1
They will learn to use topic and summing up sentences. At the same time, the teacher will show other ways of recording ideas and findings, for example by notes, lists, diagrams: 5.1.3, 5.2.1, 6.3.1

Level E: Skills of selecting facts, grouping information, emphasising key ideas, manipulating materials from more than one source, will continue to be developed: 5.3.2, 6.1.3, 6.2.1, 6.3.2

TALKING

Talking about experiences, feelings and opinions

Level D: The increased formality of the situation will require that the teacher gives support, helps pupils sort out what they want to say, how to organise it, how to use notes in planning: 5.3.4
Pupils will be asked to take account of the needs of the audience: 5.3.4

Level E: When preparing an individual talk, pupils will be helped to organise through preparation which will include research, planning, organising, identifying main ideas from supporting ideas and evidence: 5.3.4
Increasing awareness of audience will be encouraged both in selection of content and style of presentation: 5.3.4

YEAR 5 TERM 1

Focus

Year 5 Term 1 National Literacy non-fiction objectives look specifically at two forms of non-fiction writing: reports and instructions, and the technique of note-taking – a skill which children will need to master as a prerequisite to non-fiction writing of all types.

The children are given the opportunity to analyse texts of reports and instructions in discussion, noting features, style and layout, and to use these as models for their own writing.

They are encouraged to discuss the usefulness of note-taking for a range of purposes and are helped to form an individual style through use of abbreviations.

Content

Unit 1:   Reports
Unit 2:   Instructions
Unit 3:   Note-taking

Assessment

At the end of this section there are two copymasters to assess:

- Writing instructions

This copymaster is a SAT type format where the children are given starting points for a set of instructions.

- Note-taking

The children are required to read an information text and write notes using key words and abbreviations.

Curriculum Planner
National Literacy Strategy Planner

This chart shows you how to find activities by unit to resource your term's requirements for text level work on non-fiction. The learning targets closely follow the structure of the non-fiction requirements for the term in the National Literacy Strategy document (page 45). A few of the requirements are not covered.

YEAR 5 Term 1

Range

Non-fiction

- recounts of events, activities, visits, observational records, news reports, etc.
- instructional texts: rules, recipes, directions, instructions, etc., showing how things are done.

TEXT LEVEL WORK

COMPREHENSION AND COMPOSITION

Reading comprehension

Pupils should be taught:

21 to identify the features of recounted texts such as sports reports, diaries, police reports, including:

- introduction to orientate reader;
- chronological sequence;
- supporting illustrations;
- degree of formality adopted;
- use of connectives, e.g. first… next… once; Unit 1

22 to read and evaluate a range of instructional texts in terms of their:

- purposes;
- organisation and layout;
- clarity and usefulness; Unit 2

23 to discuss the purpose of note-taking and how this influences the nature of notes made; Unit 3

Writing composition

Pupils should be taught:

24 to write recounts based on subject, topic or personal experiences for (a) a close friend and (b) an unknown reader, e.g. an account of a field trip, a match, an historical event; Unit 1

25 to write instructional texts, and test them out, e.g. instructions for loading computers, design briefs for technology, rules for games; Unit 2

26 to make notes for different purposes, e.g. noting key points as a record of what has been read, listing cues for a talk, and to build on these notes in their own writing or speaking; Unit 3

27 to use simple abbreviations in note-taking; Unit 3

UNIT 1 — Reports

Learning targets

On completion of this unit the children should be able to:

1 ➤➤ identify the features of recounted texts such as sports reports, diaries, police reports, including:
  - introduction to orientate reader;
  - chronological sequence;
  - supporting illustrations;
  - degree of formality adopted;
  - use of connectives, e.g. *first...next...once*.

2 ➤➤ write recounts based on subject, topic or personal experiences for (a) a close friend and (b) an unknown reader, e.g. an account of a field trip, a match, an historical event.

Before you start

Resources for Session 1

Copymaster 1: A visit to Ordsall Hall
Copymaster 2: Report-writing frame

Resources for Session 2

Children's reports from Session 1

Assessment indicators

- Can the children write reports in a logical sequence?
- Can they alter the style of their reports according to the intended audience?

Teaching the sessions

Session 1 ① ②

Introduction | 20–25 min

▓ The children have had experience in writing newspaper reports in Year 3 so begin by asking what they understand by the term 'report'. Through discussion come to a consensus that a report can be an account of something that has happened, e.g. an event or activity, or an account of work completed, e.g. the stages of a science experiment.

Explain that a report:
- gives background information for the reader, i.e. who, what, where, when;
- relates a series of events in order;
- is usually written in the past tense.

Discuss the idea of 'audience' with the children as reports are usually written for someone else to read. Do the children think that how a report is written depends on who is going to read it?

Write the following list on the board and discuss the way each could be reported and who the children

think the intended audience might be:
- a football match;
- an educational visit to a museum;
- growing a seed in a science lesson.

Analysing a report | 15–20 min

▣ Put the children into groups and give each group copies of **Copymaster 1: A visit to Ordsall Hall**. Ask the children to read it through and make notes on each paragraph as directed by the instructions on the copymaster.

Summary | 10–15 min

▓ Discuss the report with the children, concentrating on:
- how the opening paragraph sets the scene;
- how the second paragraph gives information about what the children were going to do at the Hall;
- how the third and fourth paragraphs explain some of the things they did at the Hall;

- how the final paragraph gives extra information about the Hall and brings the reader up to date with its present usage.

Do the children think the report has been written in a sensible order?

Would they want to change the position of any of the paragraphs?

Who do they think the intended readers are?

Writing a report

`20-30min`

Give each child **Copymaster 2: Writing a report.** This is a writing framework to help them plan. They can plan a report about a school visit if one has been made recently, or an activity such as a school football or netball match. If someone has visited the school recently, e.g. the fire service, RSPB, road safety officer, etc., this could form the basis of their report. Stress that this report is going to be part of a display about the relevant activity and will be read by many people, some of whom the children may not know, e.g. visitors to the school.

Be on hand to help the children choose what they are going to write about and plan their work. They may need to be reminded of dates and important things that happened. Stress that they are writing notes at this stage and remind them about 'key words' in note-making.

Homework

The children should make a first draft of their report for you to check and discuss with them on an individual basis. This discussion is an important part of the editing and redrafting stage of their work which children find very difficult to do on their own.

Session 2 ②

Introduction

`15-20min`

This session concentrates on the aspect of 'audience' in report writing. Look again at **Copymaster 1** which the children should have concluded was written for a teacher, school magazine or to be delivered verbally to the rest of the class, etc.

Ask them to imagine that they were one of the children on this trip and that they were writing to a close friend about it. Discuss how they think the 'report' would differ and how it would be the same, e.g.

differences	similarities
a friendlier, chatty style	events still recounted in order
inclusion of personal feelings and comments	details so friend can really appreciate what the trip was like

Report for a friend

 `20min`

Ask the children to read through the report they wrote for Session 1. They are now going to rework the report as they would write it for a close friend. This is not a very realistic situation, so suggest the children think of it as a letter they might write. Encourage the children to use the same facts as in the report, emphasising that a change of audience will necessitate a change of style.

Homework

The children can copy their draft neatly, in letter format.

4

A visit to Ordsall Hall

Discuss and make notes on what each paragraph of the report tells you.

This term our class has been studying the Tudors. On the 23rd of April we went on a trip to Ordsall Hall, which is a Tudor house in Salford near Manchester.

We left school at 9.30a.m. and arrived at Ordsall Hall at 10.30a.m. We had sketch books and notebooks with us so that we could draw and make notes on the Tudor objects in the house and the decoration on the building.

Our tour of the house began in the Great Hall. The most interesting part of the Great Hall was the ceiling which was black and white. We lay down on the floor so we could sketch the patterns on the ceiling and our teacher took some photographs.

There was a lot of old furniture in the hall; large wooden chests and very uncomfortable looking chairs. It was also very draughty and we were shown a large screen which would have been used in front of a door to keep out the cold.

Ordsall Hall has been used for many things during its long history. Frederick Shields, an artist, lived there in the eighteenth century and used one room as his studio. He put in a skylight so that he had lots of light to paint by. In the nineteenth century it was used as a school to train people who wanted to become priests. The room known as the Star Chamber was where they would go to relax and chat. Today, the Hall is open to visitors and is used as a local history museum.

Report-writing frame

My report is about:

[blank box]

When it took place (date): _____

Where it took place (location): _____

_____

Why it happened (purpose): _____

_____

The order in which things happened:

_____

_____

_____

_____

_____

Others things which I would like to put in my report:

_____

_____

_____

UNIT 2 Instructions

Learning targets

On completion of this unit the children should be able to:

1 ➡➤ read and evaluate a range of instructional texts in terms of their:
   - purpose;
   - organisation and layout;
   - clarity and usefulness.

2 ➡➤ write instructional texts, and test them out, e.g. instructions for loading computers, design briefs for technology, rules for games.

Before you start

Resources for Session 1

Copymaster 3: Sort it out!
Copymaster 4: Instruction-writing frame

Links to other units

Learning Targets for Literacy Non-Fiction Years 3 and 4 Year 3 Term 2 Unit 1

Assessment indicators

- Can the children evaluate instructional texts?
- Can they write instructions in an appropriate style?

Teaching the session

Session 1 ① ②

Introduction   20 min

▨ Begin by recapping on earlier work which the children have done on instructional texts (see Links to other units). Ask for suggestions as to where the children have encountered instructions, e.g. recipes, games, for making things, etc. What can they remember about:

- how instructions are set out/organised?
- the language used, i.e. style?

Write the following on the board:

A You have to cut the yellow piece of paper into strips then stick each strip on to the red paper. You have to stick the strips on top of the red paper.

B 1. Cut the yellow piece of paper into five, 2cm wide strips.
   2. Stick the strips 1cm apart on top of the piece of red paper, using sticky tape.

Through class discussion, compare/contrast these instructions:

- Which is more precise, i.e. more detailed?
- Which is easier to follow because of the way it is set out?
- Which uses unnecessary words?

Draw the children's attention to the imperative form of the verbs in B, i.e. 'Cut' and 'Stick'. This is the verb form often used for orders. Explain that instructions are like orders in as much as you must do what the instructions tell you to achieve the desired end result.

Sort it out   20-25 min

▨ The children need **Copymaster 3: Sort it out!**, from which they must write a clear set of numbered instructions as briefly as possible. Explain that they must:

- begin with a list of what is needed;
- include all important detail;
- leave out unnecessary words;
- set out the instructions in a logical, numbered sequence.

Summary   10-20 min

▨ Ask a member of each group to read their instructions to the class. Through discussion, investigate sequence, brevity and detail. You could agree which instructions are the most clear and useful and write them on the board to form a complete set of instructions on which the children can model their individual writing.

Writing instructions ⌗30min⌗

👤 Where possible, allow the children to produce individual sets of instructions within a meaningful context, e.g. topic work, design technology briefs, loading specific software packages, etc. **Copymaster 4: Instruction-writing frame** will support the children but may need adapting for

certain types of instructions. The important point is that the children become accustomed to the style and language of instructions and can focus on key areas when planning.

Homework

The children can write neatly or word process their instructions. Where appropriate, allow some time in class to 'test' the instructions. Even if the children cannot actually carry out some of the tasks, the instructions can be discussed, focusing on the layout and detail, to assess clarity and usefulness.

Sort it out!

Read the report below on how to use the 'Learn To Spell' CD-ROM. Select the relevant information from the report to write a clear set of numbered instructions.

I have used 'Learn To Spell' on the computer and I have to write instructions so that other people in the class can use it as well.

'Learn To Spell' is a CD-ROM which you have to put into the computer. Don't put it in the slit for the floppy discs. You have to put it in the CD-ROM tray which slides out when you press the button. You have to turn on the computer first. The switch for turning on the computer is at the back on the right-hand side. The button you press is the red button on the front. When the tray slides out, you put the CD-ROM in it and press the red button again to close the tray. You have to put the CD-ROM shiny side down.

When the CD-ROM is in the tray, you will see a picture of it on the screen. You have to click on the picture. The picture comes on to the screen on the right-hand side. You have to click twice on the picture with the mouse.

When you have clicked on the picture, it will open up and show three pages. Choose the page you want and click on it. The pages are called 'Vowels', 'Blends' and 'Difficult Words'. You click twice on the one you want and follow the instructions on the screen.

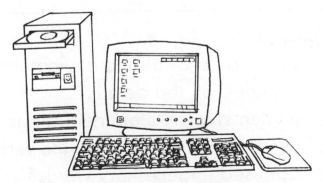

Instruction-writing frame

I am writing instructions for:

This is the equipment you need to follow these instructions:

There are ☐ steps in these instructions.

Write each step here. Give each step a number.

_____

_____

_____

_____

_____

_____

_____

_____

Have you:

- made a list of all the equipment needed?
- included all the details?
- written step-by-step instructions in the correct order?
- used the correct form of the verb in each instruction?
- not used unnecessary words?

UNIT 3 | Note-taking

Learning targets

On completion of this unit the children should be able to:

1 ➤➤ discuss the purpose of note-taking and how this influences the nature of notes made.

2 ➤➤ make notes for different purposes, e.g. noting key points as a record of what has been read, listing cues for a talk, and to build on these notes in their own writing or speaking.

3 ➤➤ use simple abbreviations in note-taking.

Before you start

Resources for Session 1

Copymaster 5: Abbreviations
Copymaster 6: Using abbreviations

Resources for Session 2

A variety of information books, encyclopedias, etc. for the children to use in research.

Links to other units

Learning Targets for Literacy: Non-Fiction Years 3 and 4 Year 3 Term 1 Unit 3 and Year 4 Term 2 Unit 1

Assessment indicators

- Can the children appreciate the reasons for being able to take notes quickly and efficiently?
- Can they recognise and use universally accepted abbreviations in their note-taking?
- Can they invent and remember personal abbreviations?
- Can they give a talk, having planned, researched and taken notes?

Teaching the sessions

Session 1 ① ③

Introduction | 20–25 min

▨ Begin by discussing with the class the purpose of note-taking. Why might they need to do it? For example:

- research – facts needed for written/oral work;
- reminders – list of things to include in letter/report, etc.

Why is it useful to begin note-taking on a given topic with listing what you already know?

Investigate the 'audience' in note-taking. Notes are usually only for the person who is writing them, to be ordered and expanded for a wider audience. Obviously, the phrase 'make notes on' can imply a more finished piece of work, but this will only serve to confuse at this stage. The important point is that the

children appreciate that note-taking is appropriate at the planning/research stage of an activity and needs to be done quickly and efficiently.

Recap on the work they have done on 'key words' (see Links to other units) and then explain that you are going to look at abbreviations which will:

- help them take notes more quickly;
- provide important links within their notes.

Give each child **Copymaster 5: Abbreviations**. Discuss what each means and how it could be useful in note-taking. The children may be interested in where the less obvious abbreviations come from:

e.g. *exempli gratia* – Latin

i.e. *id est* – Latin

N.B. *nota bene* – Latin

The blank boxes can be filled with the children's own suggestions for abbreviating words they need to use often in note-taking.

Discuss other common abbreviations which are, essentially, just a short way of writing a word, e.g.

cm	centimetre	a.m.	morning Latin – *ante meridiem*
mm	millimetre		
m	metre	p.m.	afternoon Latin – *post meridiem*
km	kilometre		
kg	kilogram	hr	hour
qr	quarter	min	minutes
pp	pages	sec	second

Using abbreviations

 20 min

Each group should have **Copymaster 6: Using abbreviations**. Each of the factual texts need to be abbreviated in note form. The children should use the abbreviation copymaster and their own abbreviations. Explain that, as note-taking is 'for their eyes only', any abbreviations/symbols they invent are fine, as long as they can remember what they mean.

Summary

10-15 min

 Compare the notes through class discussion, looking particularly at:

- areas where unnecessary words are still being used;
- effective use of universally accepted abbreviations;
- effective use of invented abbreviations.

Homework

Homework should be set when a relevant piece of note-taking is required in connection with work children are doing in class

Session 2   ②

Introduction

20-30 min

 This session requires the children to research and make notes in preparation for giving a talk to the class on a subject which interests them.

Explain to the children that they are not going to write out every word which they will say, but make

notes under headings so that they can refer to them as they go along.

The children will need a model to do the research and planning for this activity so choose a common subject such as 'bicycles' and take them through the various stages:

1 Write the title of the talk in the middle of a sheet of paper. (You write on the board.)
2 Think of the different areas and aspects of the topic you can talk about and, using the children's suggestions, draw a web:

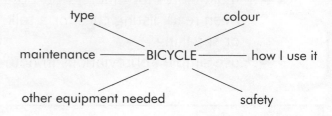

The children will suggest areas which they know something about, so add an area about which they would have to research and make notes, e.g. a brief history of the bicycle.

Take each section of the web and ask the children what they would say about it, e.g.

Other equipment needed: safety helmet, bicycle pump, puncture repair kit, etc.

Discuss the research aspect, reminding them about using indexes and contents pages to locate information, and note-taking using key words and abbreviations.

Preparing a talk (this could require several sessions and homework time)

Be on hand to help the children in:

- choosing their topic;
- brainstorming;
- ensuring there is an element of research included;
- taking notes efficiently;
- putting their notes in a logical sequence under headings.

Ensure that each day, 2 or 3 children are given the opportunity to present their talk to the class.

5 | Abbreviations

& / +   and

incl.   including

gd   good

e.g.   for example

i.e.   that is

etc.   and so on

∴   therefore

∵   because

no.   number

NB   of particular importance

Using abbreviations

Both plants and animals need water to survive. Most plants take water from the soil through their roots. Animals drink water.

Plants need sunlight as well as water. Plants change sunlight directly into energy which they use to grow and produce new plant material such as leaves.

Animals need sunlight for different reasons; it provides the heat and light which they need to live. Animals cannot change sunlight into energy like plants do, so many animals eat plants to get the energy they need to live.

Make your notes here: _____

_____

_____

_____

Iron ore is a mineral which is dug from the ground. It can then be melted down and made into sheets of steel. These sheets can be made into things such as cars, cookers and aeroplanes.

Oil is found far underground in certain areas. Oil companies drill down into the ground and bring the oil to the surface. It can be made into many things; petrol for cars and lorries, and plastic for things such as toys and bin liners.

Clay is also found in the ground. We can use it to make things such as pots and bricks. The clay is shaped and then fired (heated to a high temperature) to make the finished object.

Make your notes here: _____

_____

_____

_____

Choose **one** of the following starting points:

Imagine a Martian has landed in your garden. You get on really well and show the Martian around your house and give him something to eat and drink.

When the time comes for him to return to Mars, he asks you how you made what he has eaten or drunk.

Write a clear set of instructions for the Martian, including ingredients, equipment and how you made it.

Here is a sum where hundreds, tens and units have been added:

$$
\begin{array}{ccc}
H & T & U \\
5 & 9 & 2 \\
+\; 1_1 & 3_1 & 9 \\
\hline
7 & 3 & 1 \\
\hline
\end{array}
$$

Write clear, step-by-step instructions for someone who does not know how to do this type of sum.

Reading comprehension/Writing composition
Taking notes

Read through the information passage on Ancient Egyptian food.
Make notes using key words and abbreviations.

> The basic Egyptian diet was bread, beer, vegetables and fresh or dried
> fish. Even the poor ate this.
>
> The vegetables which were available to the Ancient Egyptians
> included leeks, onions, cucumber, lettuce, garlic, beans and lentils.
>
> Fruit was usually reserved for feasts and was most often figs, dates,
> melons and grapes.
>
> Meat was a real luxury but on special occasions pigeon, duck, goose,
> beef, goat or pork would be cooked.
>
> There was a good range of cakes and, of course, bread was an
> important part of the diet. It was made from wholemeal flour, salt and
> water.
>
> Beer was the most common drink and some sorts had wonderful
> names such as 'the joy bringer' and 'the heavenly'. Both beer and wine
> were made locally but also imported along with olive oil and spices.

Make your notes here:

_____

_____

_____

_____

_____

_____

_____

_____

_____

YEAR 5 TERM 2

Focus

Year 5 Term 2 National Literacy non-fiction objectives concentrate on explanatory texts, i.e. the understanding and writing of processes. The children are given the opportunity to analyse explanatory texts in discussion, noting features, style and layout, and to use this as a model for their own writing.

Note-taking is expanded to include the idea of children acknowledging where they have found information through compiling bibliographies and incorporating and acknowledging quotations within their own written work.

Content

Unit 1: Explanatory texts
Unit 2: Acknowledging sources

Assessment

Copymaster 15 assesses the children's ability to transfer diagrammatic information of a process into an explanatory text using impersonal style, technical language, passive voice and linking words and phrases.

Curriculum Planner
National Literacy Strategy Planner

This chart shows you how to find activities by unit to resource your term's requirements for text level work on non-fiction. The learning targets closely follow the structure of the non-fiction requirements for the term in the National Literacy Strategy document (page 47). A few of the requirements are not covered.

YEAR 5 Term 2

Range

Non-fiction

- non-chronological reports (i.e. to describe and classify);
- explanations (processes, systems, operations, etc.).

Use content from other subjects, e.g. how the digestive system works, how to find a percentage, the rain cycle, etc.

TEXT LEVEL WORK

COMPREHENSION AND COMPOSITION

Reading comprehension

Pupils should be taught:

15 to read a range of explanatory texts, investigating and noting features of impersonal style, e.g. complex sentences: use of passive voice; technical vocabulary; hypothetical language (*if…then, might when the…*); use of words/phrases to make sequential, causal, logical connections, e.g. *while, during, after, because, due to, only when, so*; Unit 1

18 how authors record and acknowledge their sources; Unit 2

20 notemaking: to discuss what is meant by 'in your own words' and when it is appropriate to copy, quote and adapt; Unit 2

Writing composition

Pupils should be taught:

21 to convert personal notes into notes for others to read, paying attention to appropriateness of style, vocabulary and presentation; Unit 1

22 to plan, compose, edit and refine short non-chronological reports and explanatory texts, using reading as a source, focusing on clarity, conciseness, and impersonal style; Unit 1

23 to record and acknowledge sources in their own writing; Unit 2

UNIT 1 | Explanatory texts

Learning targets

On completion of this unit the children should be able to:

1 ➤➤ read a range of explanatory texts, investigating and noting features of impersonal style, e.g. complex sentences: use of passive voice; technical vocabulary; hypothetical language (*if...then, might when the...*); use of words/phrases to make sequential, causal, logical connections, e.g. *while, during, after, because, due to, only when, so.*

2 ➤➤ convert personal notes into notes for others to read, paying attention to appropriateness of style, vocabulary and presentation.

3 ➤➤ plan, compose, edit and refine short non-chronological reports and explanatory texts, using reading as a source, focusing on clarity, conciseness, and impersonal style.

Before you start

Resources for Session 1

Copymaster 9: The digestive system
Copymaster 10: How do we hear?
Copymaster 11: Analysing an explanatory text

Resources for Session 2

Copymaster 12: Writing to explain

Links to other units

Learning Targets for Literacy: Non-Fiction Years 3 and 4 Year 4 Term 2 Unit 3

Assessment indicators

*   Can the children identify an explanatory text?
*   Can they note and comment on the features of an explanatory text?
*   Can they plan, draft and edit an explanatory text using common features?

Teaching the sessions

Session 1 ①

Introduction [20–25 min]

▨ Begin by giving each child **Copymaster 9: The digestive system**. Read through it and discuss the purpose of the writing, i.e. does it:

*   give instructions;
*   tell a story;
*   put forward an opinion;
*   persuade;
*   explain?

They should see that the text is explaining how something happens (a process). What do they understand by the term 'process'?

Discuss in what other way this information could have been presented, i.e. annotated diagram. If necessary recap on earlier explanatory text work. (see Links to other units.)

Use the text to highlight the following features of explanatory texts:

*   impersonal style. Draw the children's attention to the fact that the text does not say:
    our/your/my mouth – it says 'the mouth'
    our/your/my body – it says 'the body'
    my breakfast/lunch – it says 'the food'

*   use of technical language:
    'digestive process'
    'gullet'
    'enzymes'
    'small intestine'
    'large intestine'

- passive voice:
  '…which begin to digest it'
  '…water is absorbed'
- words/phrases which move the reader from one part of the process to another in a logical sequence:
  'The first stage…'
  'The second stage…'
  'During this process…'
  'The food then passes…'
  'When the body…'

Analysing an explanatory text 20min

The children should read and discuss **Copymaster 10: How do we hear?. Copymaster 11: Analysing explanatory texts** gives the children a framework for looking at the text and noting logical sequence and important features.

Summary 10min

The children can compare their findings through class discussion and investigate the possible advantages of having a labelled/annotated diagram to go with the text. What do the children think is the best way to present an explanatory text? As a:

- text;
- text and labelled diagram;
- text and annotated diagram;
- annotated diagram?

Homework

The children should think carefully and make notes about a process with which they are familiar or can easily research, in preparation for the next session.

Session 2

Introduction 20min

This session is devoted to the children planning, composing, editing and refining an explanatory text of their, or your choosing. **Copymaster 12: Writing to explain** will be useful to the children in their planning and editing stages.

- Check what each child has chosen to write about to ensure that it does require an explanatory text as opposed to a set of instructions, etc. Wherever possible, steer the children to relevant topic work but have as much variety as possible.
- Discuss with the class how they will begin, i.e. making notes, ordering, checking spelling/meanings of unfamiliar technical terms, etc.
- Ask each child to fill in **Copymaster 12** so that you can check at the planning stage that they are on the right track.

Writing your explanation 30min

This can be attempted in a group or pairs if you feel the children need collaborative support for this initial attempt. However the activity is organised, a first draft should be produced and discussed with you, using the check-list at the bottom of the copymaster as a guide.

Once you are both satisfied that the draft meets the criteria for explanatory texts, it can be written neatly or word processed. If any child wishes to include an annotated/labelled diagram, this would be a good opportunity for them to do some design work on computer or, if possible, to scan in a relevant diagram.

Mount a display of the finished work under the heading 'Processes' or 'Explanatory Writing'.

The digestive system

Digestion means the breaking down of food so that the body can absorb and use it. Food is broken down in two stages:

The first stage is when the food is chewed in the mouth. This part of the digestive process is quite quick.

The second stage takes much longer and begins when the food passes down the gullet from the mouth.

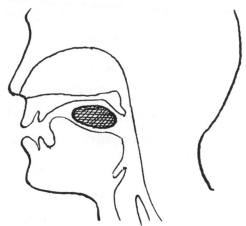

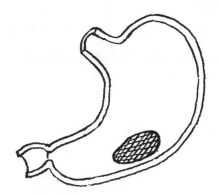

The food first enters the stomach and mixes with enzymes which begin to digest it. During this process, if any germs have entered the stomach with the food, they are killed.

The food then passes through the small intestine. Enzymes continue the digestive process and some of the digested food passes through the gut wall into the blood.

The food then passes into the large intestine where water is absorbed which the body needs.

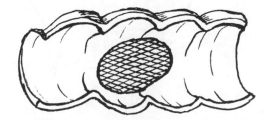

When the body has taken what it needs from the food, the remaining waste material passes into the rectum and is expelled from the body.

How do we hear?

When something moves and makes a sound, the sound is heard by the ear because of sound waves.

The movement of an object is called vibration. This vibration then makes the air vibrate, producing sound waves.

These sound waves pass through the air and into the ear. When the waves reach the ear-drum, they make it vibrate and, in turn, the small bones in the ear vibrate.

The vibration then passes through the semi-circular canals in the ear to the cochlea. The cochlea is covered in tiny hairs. These hairs pick up the vibration and pass it through to the auditory nerve.

Finally, the auditory nerve, which is connected directly to the brain, sends a message to the brain. This message is translated by the brain into the sound which was made.

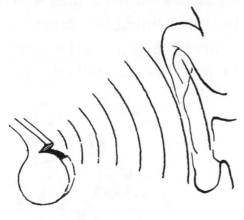

Sound waves moving
towards ear

The cochlea and auditory
nerve

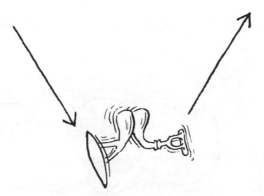

Vibration of ear-drum
and small bones in ear

11 | Analysing an explanatory text

What process is the
text explaining?

How many paragraphs
are there?

Summarise each paragraph in a few words:

_____

_____

_____

_____

_____

Find examples of:

impersonal style:

technical language:

passive voice:

words/phrases used
to help the reader
move logically
through the process:

Writing to explain

The process I am describing is:

The numbered stages in the process:

_____   _____

_____   _____

_____   _____

_____   _____

How many paragraphs will you need?

Technical words/phrases in the process and what they mean:

_____   _____

_____   _____

_____   _____

_____   _____

Write your first draft then check:

- you have written a logical sequence from the beginning of the process to the end;

- you have helped your reader move from stage to stage by using such words/phrases as: firstly, the next stage, after this, when, during, etc.

- you have written in an impersonal style, e.g. 'the food' not 'my food'

- you have sometimes used the passive voice, e.g. 'The worm is then eaten by the bird' instead of 'The bird eats the worm'.

Acknowledging sources

Learning targets

On completion of this unit the children should be able to:

1 ➤➤ identify how authors record and acknowledge their sources.
2 ➤➤ notemaking: to discuss what is meant by 'in your own words' and when it is appropriate to copy, quote and adapt.
3 ➤➤ record and acknowledge sources in their own writing.

Before you start

Resources for Session 1

Copymaster 13: Native shrubs and trees
Copymaster 14: Acknowledging sources
Groups of books (at least 3 in each group) on the same/similar topic

Assessment indicators

- Can the children identify ways in which writers acknowledge their sources?
- Can they use these ways to acknowledge sources in their own work?

Teaching the sessions

Session 1 ① ② ③

Introduction   20-25 min

▓ The children have had experience of note-taking to research a topic, using information books, CD-ROMs, etc. This unit builds on this skill and introduces the idea of acknowledging where information has been found.

Give each child **Copymaster 13: Native shrubs and trees**, and explain to the children that the writer had to:

- research the topic;
- make notes;
- keep a list of the books used;
- write up the notes into a non-chronological report.

Read through the copymaster with the children and discuss:

- the use of quotes within the text

  Quotes are the actual words in the information book which the writer wants to use. They must be written in the report in quotation marks, i.e. speech marks. You cannot just copy someone else's work without acknowledging that the words are not yours. The best way to do this is to number each quote and write at the end of the report where these words come from.

  Ask the children to find the quotes in the report and say where they come from. The quotes are deliberately from the same source to show the children that they do not have to write out the source each time. If two consecutive quotes come from the same source then you can write 'ibid' which means 'in the same place'.

- the bibliography

  This is a list of books which the writer has used in researching the topic. It is arranged in alphabetical order by the surname of the author. This is followed by the title, which is underlined, the publisher and the date when the book was published. Ask the children:

- how many books the writer consulted in putting together this report?
- the authors of the books in the bibliography?
- the publishers of the books in the bibliography?
- which is the most recent book consulted?
- which is the oldest book consulted?

Acknowledging sources 20min

Put the children into small groups or pairs and explain that they are going to begin researching a given topic. The topic will depend on the group of books which they have, e.g. one pair might be researching Elizabeth I and their books will all be relevant to this.

Give each group/pair **Copymaster 14: Acknowledging sources**. They have to:

- list the books as they would appear in a bibliography;
- find two quotes they would like to use in their non-chronological report, copy them out, number them and record the sources.

Ensure the children have **Copymaster 13** on hand on which to model their work.

Summary 10min

Use this time to correct any organisational mistakes you have noticed as the children have been working and to discuss any difficulties the children may be having.

Using the library 20-30min

If possible, use current topic work as the basis of this activity. The children should use the school/class library to make a list of books which they could use for a given topic. The list should then be arranged as it would appear in a bibliography if all the books were used for a non-chronological report.

13 Native shrubs and trees

'Native trees and shrubs are those that arrive in this country naturally without being introduced either on purpose or accidentally.'[1]

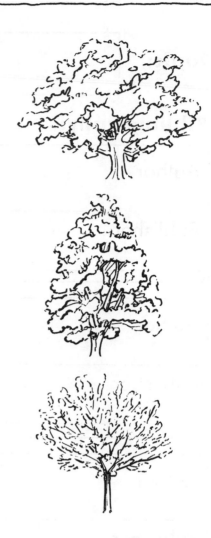

Native plants have been here for a very long time and we are used to seeing them around us in our landscape. Examples of native shrubs and trees are oak, willow, birch and elm.

The alder tree is native to this country and is usually found near water. It has broad leaves and cones. Birds such as reed buntings and tree creepers feed on the seeds inside the cones.

Native trees and shrubs are very useful for wildlife. 'Over a very long time more and more insects have developed to be able to make use of these trees and shrubs.'[2] Trees and shrubs which have been introduced to this country have fewer insects which live off them. For example, the flowering Japanese cherry has been introduced to this country but the insects which live off it are still in Japan and cannot survive here.

1 STEP 5 – 16 Design and Technology, edited by Howard Bagshaw, published by Cambridge University Press, 1991.

2 ibid.

Bibliography

Bagshaw, H. STEP 5 – 16 Design and Technology, published by Cambridge University Press, 1991.

Black, F. Trees and shrubs, published by The Green Press, 1997.

Selberg, I. The Usborne Nature Trail Book of Trees and Leaves, published by Usborne, 1977.

14 | Acknowledging sources

Topic:

Bibliography:

Author _____   Title _____

Publisher _____   Date _____

Author _____   Title _____

Publisher _____   Date _____

Author _____   Title _____

Publisher _____   Date _____

Quotations:

_____

Number [＿＿＿]   Source

Number [＿＿＿]   Source

Writing composition
Explanatory texts

Here is a diagram showing what happens when we breathe:

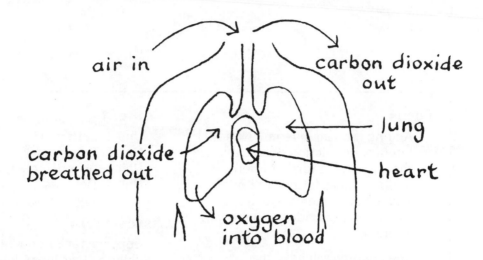

Use the space below to write an explanation of what happens when we breathe. Continue on the back of the copymaster if you need more space.

Remember:
- impersonal style
- use of technical language
- passive voice
- words/phrases which move the reader from one stage of the process to the next.

_____

_____

_____

_____

_____

_____

_____

YEAR 5 TERM 3

Focus

Among the Year 5 Term 3 National Literacy non-fiction objectives there are three forms of non-fiction writing: letters, editorials and advertisements which are written to persuade in one way or another.

The children will have the opportunity to analyse each type of persuasive writing through discussion, noting features, style and layout, and to use these as models for their own writing.

The objectives also stipulate that children should be able to present an argument or point of view orally, and Unit 4 concentrates on how formal and balloon debates are arranged.

Content

Unit 1: Letters
Unit 2: Editorials
Unit 3: Advertisements
Unit 4: Debates

Assessment

Copymaster 31 and 32 give the children starting points for assessing their ability to write

- letters of complaint;
- persuasive letters;
- editorials.

Curriculum Planner
National Literacy Strategy Planner

This chart shows you how to find activities by unit to resource your term's requirements for text level work on non-fiction. The learning targets closely follow the structure of the non-fiction requirements for the term in the National Literacy Strategy document (page 49). A few of the requirements are not covered.

YEAR 5   Term 3

Range

Non-fiction

- persuasive writing to put or argue a point of view: including letters and commentaries to persuade, criticise, protest, support, object, complain;
- dictionaries, thesauruses, including IT sources.

TEXT LEVEL WORK

COMPREHENSION AND COMPOSITION

Reading comprehension

Pupils should be taught:

12 to read and evaluate letters, e.g. from newspapers, magazines, intended to inform, protest, complain, persuade, considering (i) how they are set out (ii) how language is used, e.g. to gain attention, respect, manipulate; Unit 1, Unit 3

13 to read other examples, e.g. newspaper comment, headlines, adverts, fliers. Compare writing which informs and persuades, considering, e.g.
- the deliberate use of ambiguity, half-truth, bias
- how opinion can be disguised to seem like fact; Unit 2

14 to select and evaluate a range of texts, in print or other media, for persuasiveness, clarity, quality of information; Unit 1, Unit 2, Unit 3

15 from reading, to collect and investigate use of persuasive devices:
e.g. words and phrases: e.g. 'surely', 'it wouldn't be very difficult…'; persuasive definitions, e.g. 'no-one but a complete idiot…', 'every right thinking person would…', 'the real truth is…'; rhetorical questions: 'are we expected to..?', 'where will future audiences come from..?'; pandering, condescension, concession etc.; 'Naturally, it takes time for local residents…'; deliberate ambiguities, e.g. 'probably the best…in the world', 'known to cure all…', 'the professionals' choice'; Unit 1, Unit 2, Unit 3

Writing composition

17 to draft and write individual, group or class letters for real purposes, e.g. put a point of view, comment on an emotive issue, protest; to edit and present to finished state; Unit 1

18 to write a commentary on an issue on paper or screen, (e.g. as a news editorial, leaflet), setting out and justifying a personal view; to use structures from reading to set out and link points, e.g. numbered lists, bullet points; Unit 2

19 construct an argument in note form or full text to persuade others of a point of view and:
- present the case to the class or a group;
- evaluate its effectiveness; Unit 4

UNIT 1 | Letters

Learning targets

On completion of this unit the children should be able to:

1 ➤ read and evaluate letters, e.g. from newspapers, magazines, intended to inform, protest, complain, persuade, considering: (i) how they are set out (ii) how language is used, e.g. to gain attention, respect, manipulate.

2 ➤ select and evaluate a range of texts, in print or other media, for persuasiveness, clarity, quality of information.

3 ➤ from reading, to collect and investigate use of persuasive devices: e.g. words and phrases: e.g. *'surely'*, *'it wouldn't be very difficult...'*; persuasive definitions, e.g. *'no-one but a complete idiot...'*, *'every right thinking person would...'*, *'the real truth is...'*; rhetorical questions: *'are we expected to..?'*, *'where will future audiences come from..?'*; pandering, condescension, concession etc.; *'Naturally, it takes time for local residents...'*; deliberate ambiguities, e.g. *'probably the best...in the world'*, *'known to cure all...'*, *'the professionals' choice'*.

4 ➤ draft and write individual, group or class letters for real purposes, e.g. put a point of view, comment on an emotive issue, protest; to edit and present to finished state.

Before you start

Resources for Session 1

Copymaster 16: A letter of complaint 1
Copymaster 17: A letter of complaint 2
Copymaster 18: Writing letters of complaint
Copymaster 19: Letter of complaint writing frame

Resources for Session 2

Copymaster 20: A persuasive letter 1
Copymaster 21: A persuasive letter 2
Copymaster 22: Writing letters to persuade
Copymaster 23: Persuasive letter-writing frame

Links to other units

Learning Targets for Literacy: Non-Fiction Years 3 and 4
Year 3 Term 3 Unit 1, Year 4 Term 3 Unit 1

Assessment indicators

- Can the children read and evaluate letters which are written for a specific purpose?
- Can they write formal letters for a specific purpose, using tone, style and vocabulary appropriately?

Teaching the sessions

Session 1 ① ② ④

Introduction   15–20 min

▨ The children have had experience of writing informal letters with the emphasis on accepted layout and the need for clarity of purpose and organisation. Recap on why we write 'friendly' letters and expand the discussion into other types of letters we might write and to whom.

Explain to the children that in these sessions they are going to investigate and compose 'formal' letters. They may be more familiar with the term 'business letters'. Ask them to help you compile a list of types of formal letter. Ensure that the variety listed in the

NLS objectives are included.

Once the list has been compiled, ask the children to suggest examples of what the content of each type of letter might be:

letter type	examples of content
inform	information about: products, opening and closing times, prices, availability, etc.
protest	protesting about: treatment of animals, building on open space, closing of local amenities, etc.
complain	complaining about: noise, traffic, pollution, something that adversely affects the writer, etc.
persuade	to persuade the reader about what should or should not be done by a local council, government, the police, etc.

Have the children (probably through their families) had any experience of such letters?

Analysing letters of complaint

 Give each group **Copymaster 16: A letter of complaint 1**. They should read and discuss the letter, answering the questions at the bottom of the copymaster in preparation for a class discussion on style and content.

Summary

Compare the children's answers through class discussion. Questions 1–6 and 8 should have illicited a 'no' response, and Question 7, a 'yes' response.

Discuss in general terms what they think of the letter and how well it fulfils its intended purpose.

Analysing letters of complaint

Copymaster 17: A letter of complaint 2, gives the children another letter with which they can compare the first one. They should discuss it in groups, considering the following:

- the inclusion of addresses – why is it important? How does this aspect of letter 2 differ from an informal letter?
- the ending – how should this differ from an informal letter? Explain that you use 'faithfully' when you do not know the name of the person you are writing to and 'sincerely' when you do.
- the organisation – which letter clearly states the problem, the exact nature of the complaint and the action the writer has taken to address the problem?
- the tone – although both are letters of complaint, which letter adopts a reasonable tone; which letter is designed to get a favourable response?
- the vocabulary – which letter uses formal 'business-like' vocabulary?

Summary

Compare the children's views on the two letters through class discussion, investigating particularly:

- why a letter of complaint is written, i.e. to have something done about the situation;
- how you want the reader of a letter of complaint to respond, i.e. to do something about the situation;
- the formal language, e.g.

'As you are no doubt aware'	(I think you probably know)
'as a consequence'	(because of this)
'infrequent bus service'	(the buses don't run very often)
'lack of this service'	(there isn't one)
'Initially'	(at first)
'in this instance'	(over this problem)
'totally inadequate'	(rubbish!)

Writing a letter of complaint

Copymaster 18: Writing letters of complaint, gives the children various scenarios on which to write and **Copymaster 19: Letter of complaint writing frame** will give structured support to those children who need it for making initial notes. Encourage the children to write in draft, modelling their work on **Copymaster 17**, and discuss their letters individually at this stage.

Homework

The children should make a neat copy by writing or word processing their letter. As a follow-up homework the children could swap letters and write a formal reply indicating what they intend to do about the complaint.

Session 2

Introduction

This session follows the format of Session 1 but takes the children on from letters which just 'complain' to letters which seek to persuade the reader to adopt the point of view or course of action proposed by the writer.

The children have had experience of writing to persuade in a different context (see Links to other units) but it is worth recapping on what they understand by 'persuasion'. In what form does 'persuasion' most often enter daily life? (Advertising.)

Analysing persuasive letters 1 `15 min`

♣ Give each group **Copymaster 20: A persuasive letter 1**. They should read and discuss the letter, answering the questions at the bottom of the copymaster in preparation for a class discussion on style and content.

Summary `10 min`

▦ Compare the children's answers through class discussion. All questions should have illicited a 'no' response.

How would the children correct the opening and ending of the letter?

> opening: Dear Sir or Madam
>
> ending: Yours faithfully

Discuss in general terms what they think of the letter and how well it fulfils its intended purpose.

Analysing persuasive letters 2 `15-20 min`

♣ **Copymaster 21: A persuasive letter 2**, gives the children another letter with which they can compare the first one. They should discuss it in groups, considering the following:

- the inclusion of addresses – why is it important and how does this aspect of letter 2 differ from an informal letter?
- the ending – how should this differ from an informal letter?
- the opening paragraph – why does the writer begin by pointing out the things the council has done well?
- the organisation – which letter clearly states the problem, gives valid reasons which would persuade the reader that the problem should be addressed and gives helpful suggestions as to what to do?
- the tone – although both are letters hoping to persuade the reader to take a course of action, which letter adopts a really persuasive tone? Which letter is designed to get a favourable response?
- the vocabulary – which letter uses formal 'business-like' vocabulary and persuasive words and phrases?

Summary `10-15 min`

▦ Compare the children's views on the two letters through class discussion, investigating particularly:

- why a persuasive letter is written, i.e. to persuade someone to do something;
- how you want the reader of a persuasive letter to respond, i.e. to be persuaded of your point of view and act upon it;
- the formal language, e.g.

'excellent facilities'	(good things which people use)
'this situation is rectified'	(something is done about it)
'a vast increase'	(lots more)
'designated playing area'	(somewhere just for children to play)
'three possible locations'	(three places which could be used as a park or playing field)
'effect a change of use'	(make them into a park or playing field)

- the persuasive language, e.g.

'it is essential that'	(it is really important that)
'for a variety of reasons'	(for many different reasons)
'Surely..'	(you must agree with me…)
'is a danger'	(it is dangerous and could cause an accident)
'play in safety'	(play somewhere safe)
'are in favour'	(agree with this)

Writing a persuasive letter `20-30 min`

👤 **Copymaster 22: Writing letters to persuade**, gives the children various scenarios on which to write and **Copymaster 23: Persuasive letter-writing frame** will give structured support to those children who need it for making initial notes. Encourage the children to write in draft, modelling their work on **Copymaster 21**, and discuss their letters individually at this stage.

Homework

The children should make a neat copy by writing or word processing their letter. As a follow-up homework the children could swap letters and write a formal reply indicating how much they were persuaded by the letter.

17th December

Dear Sir or Madam,

I am really fed up with not being able to get out of my road in the morning. You should be able to do something about it. After all, you are the local council and I pay my council tax just like everyone else.

It isn't good enough! What am I supposed to do? Get up at the crack of dawn and use a spade? I expect a reply to my letter immediately and something done by tomorrow morning or I will come down to the council offices and make real trouble.

I am very angry,
Mr B. Warned

You are a local councillor and have just received this letter.
Answer 'Yes' or 'No' to these questions.

1 Do you know where Mr B. Warned lives?

2 Can you reply to his letter?

3 Can you ring him up?

4 Do you know exactly what his problem is?

5 Can you solve it?

6 Does the letter make you want to help him?

7 Does the letter make you angry?

8 Is this a good way to write a letter to complain about something?

5, Beech Lane
Slugsville
Lancashire
17th December

Slugsville Council
The Town Hall
Slugsville

Dear Sir or Madam,

I live in a small cottage in Beech Lane, a narrow cul-de-sac on the edge of the town.

As you are no doubt aware, over the past few days there have been heavy snowfalls and, as a consequence, Beech Lane has been totally blocked. I have been unable to get my car down the lane and, with the infrequent bus service in my part of town, getting to work has proved very difficult.

Snow ploughs and gritting lorries have been at work in other parts of the town and so I felt that I had to write to complain about the lack of this service where I live.

Initially, I assumed you were unaware of the state of Beech Lane so I rang the council offices on 15th December to be told that a snow plough would be sent out immediately. Two days have now passed and the lane is still blocked.

As a council tax payer, I feel the service you are providing in this instance is totally inadequate and I hope you will not think me unreasonable for demanding that this situation be attended to as soon as possible.

Yours faithfully,

Mr B. Reasonable

Writing letters of complaint

Choose **one** of the following situations and write a letter of complaint.

You live in a small village where there is only one bus a week to the nearest town. For the past few weeks the bus has either arrived very late or has not turned up at all.

Write to Mrs Driver who is the person in the council responsible for public transport.

The roof in your school is leaking. No one from the Building Services Department has visited the school to see what needs doing even though the Head Teacher has rung up several times.

Write a letter to the Building Services Department complaining about how the situation is affecting you.

You sent away for a game for your computer and when it arrived it would not work. You sent it back asking for a replacement but you have heard nothing.

Write to the Managing Director of the company 'Games Are Us' complaining about their service.

Letter of complaint writing frame

address of sender:

address to which the
letter is being sent:

date:

opening:

First paragraph, introducing yourself:

Second paragraph, indicating what you are complaining about:

Final paragraph, saying what you would like done about your complaint:

Formal ending:

A persuasive letter 1

14th June

Dear Sir,

Our village does not have a playing field or a park. The local people have been asking for you to do something about this for many years. We are still waiting. The village two miles down the road has a park which you provided so why can't you do the same for us?

Hope to hear from you soon,
Mrs I. Want

You are a local councillor and have just received this letter.
Answer 'yes' or 'no' to these questions.

1 Do you know which village Mrs I. Want is writing about?

2 Can you reply to this letter?

3 Does this letter give you any reasons why the village should have a playing field or park?

4 Does this letter persuade you that the village should have a playing field or park?

5 Is the letter set out as a formal letter should be?

6 The writer does not know the name of the person to whom she is writing.

a. Is the opening correct?

b. Is the ending correct?

The Hollows
Elm Lane
Dagglewood
Flintshire
DW4 9SH

14th June

Flintshire Council
Council Offices
Mold
MD3 8FL

Dear Sir or Madam,

      I have lived in the village of Dagglewood for many years. It is a delightful spot with three shops, a pub, a good bus service and excellent facilities for older people.

The one thing that Dagglewood lacks is a park or playing field for the children of the village and I feel it is essential that this situation is rectified as soon as possible for a variety of reasons.

Several small estates have been built on the edge of the village over recent years and there are now many more children of all ages in the village. Surely, somewhere for our youngsters to play is not an unreasonable request?

Dagglewood stands at the foot of Flint Mountain, a tourist attraction, and the summer months see a vast increase in the amount of traffic which comes along the main street. This traffic is a danger to children who have to play in the streets and lanes because there is no designated playing area.

A park or playing field would give a focal point to the village where children could play in safety and local village events could take place.

I enclose a sketch map of the village and surrounding area, with three possible locations marked. Two of the suggested sites are already council property so it would not be very difficult to effect a change of use. I also enclose a petition signed by 82% of the people who live in the village and are in favour of such an amenity being provided.

I look forward to hearing from you in the near future.

      Yours faithfully,
      Mrs I. Need

Choose **one** of the following situations and write a letter to persuade.

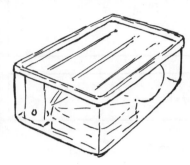

You wish to persuade the Governors of your school to allow you to have packed lunches. At the moment, you have to either stay for school dinners or go home for lunch.

Write a letter to your Governors to persuade them that packed lunches are a good idea.

Your youth club wants to do a sponsored walk for charity. Part of the route is across fields that belong to a local farmer. You have heard that he is not keen on the idea of lots of people walking across his land.

Write a letter to the farmer to persuade him to give you permission to cross his land.

There are no recycling bins in the area where you live. You want bins where you can put plastic, glass and paper.

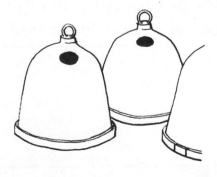

Write a letter to your local council that would persuade them to install bins near the shopping area.

Persuasive letter-writing frame

address of sender:

address to which the
letter is being sent:

date:

opening:

First paragraph, introducing yourself and what you are writing about:

Body of the letter, giving clear reasons for what you are proposing:

Final paragraph, giving helpful suggestions as to how what you are proposing can be done:

Formal ending:

Editorials

Learning targets

On completion of this unit the children should be able to:

1 ➡ read other examples, e.g. newspaper comment, headlines, adverts, fliers. Compare writing which informs and persuades, considering, e.g.
   - the deliberate use of ambiguity, half truth, bias;
   - how opinion can be disguised to seem like fact.

2 ➡ select and evaluate a range of texts, in print or other media, for persuasiveness, clarity, quality of information.

3 ➡ from reading, to collect and investigate use of persuasive devices: e.g. words and phrases: e.g. *'surely'*, *'it wouldn't be very difficult...'*; persuasive definitions, e.g. *'no-one but a complete idiot...'*, *'every right thinking person would...'*, *'the real truth is...'*; rhetorical questions: *'are we expected to..?'*, *'where will future audiences come from..?'*; pandering, condescension, concession, etc.; *'Naturally, it takes time for local residents...'*; deliberate ambiguities, e.g. *'probably the best...in the world'*, *'known to cure all...'*, *'the professionals' choice'*.

4 ➡ write a commentary on an issue on paper or screen, (e.g. as a news editorial, leaflet), setting out and justifying a personal view; to use structures from reading to set out and link points, e.g. numbered lists, bullet points.

Before you start

Resources for Session 1

Copymaster 24: Front page story
Copymaster 25: Editorial
Copymaster 26: Editorial writing frame

Resources for Session 2

The children's work from Session 1

Links to other units

Learning Targets for Literacy: Non-Fiction Years 3 and 4 Year 3 Term 3 Unit 2, Year 4 Term 1 Unit 2, Year 4 Term 1 Unit 3, Year 4 Term 3 Unit 1, Year 4 Term 3 Unit 3

Assessment indicators

- Can the children recognise persuasive text?
- Can they plan and write a persuasive text in the style of a newspaper editorial?

Teaching the sessions

Session 1 ① ② ③

Introduction 10–15 min

▧ Following on from the 'letters to persuade' in the previous unit, explain to the children that they are going to look at an aspect of newspapers that is designed to persuade the reader to agree with a particular point of view.

Begin by recapping on what the children have learned

about newspapers (see Links to other units) and introduce them to the term 'editorial'. This is an article in a newspaper, usually written by the editor, which adopts a particular point of view on a current news story and seeks to persuade the reader to agree with that point of view.

Investigating editorials 15–20 min

▧ Give each group **Copymaster 24: Front page story**, and **Copymaster 25: Editorial**. Explain to the children that these articles are from the same local newspaper. **Copymaster 24** revises the presentation of fact and opinion. **Copymaster 25** is an example of how one side of an argument is presented. They should read and discuss them, making notes at the bottom of each copymaster in preparation for a class discussion.

Summary
`15-20min`

Discuss **Copymaster 24: Front page story** in terms of the facts and opinions presented. Introduce and explain the terms 'bias' and 'even-handedness' and investigate which is an accurate description of this article. In simple terms, is the writer giving equal weight to both sides of the argument, or is it obvious which side of the argument the writer is on?

Discuss **Copymaster 25: Editorial** in terms of 'bias' and 'even-handedness':

- Does the writer look at both sides of the argument?
- Does the writer ignore one side of the argument?
- Does the writer present facts that allow the readers to make up their own minds?

Discuss the organisation of the editorial, looking at each paragraph to select key words and phrases and how they are linked, i.e.

Paragraph 1: brief introduction of the issue

Paragraph 2: those responsible for the action

Paragraph 3: those affected by the action – town centre shopkeepers

Paragraph 4: those affected by the action – shoppers

Paragraph 5: an appeal to agree with the editorial opinion

Paragraph 6: an invitation to positive action

Discuss the use of language in the editorial, investigating the effect of:

'Surely it is time…'

'Every right thinking person can see this.'

'it is about time…'

'The real truth is…'

'It is time to make a stand…'

Planning an editorial
`20min`

This planning activity can be tackled in pairs or individually. Give the children **Copymaster 26: Editorial writing frame**, and explain that they are going to begin thinking and planning an editorial for an imaginary local newspaper.

Spend some time with the whole class discussing the headings on the copymaster:

- Issue: this is the subject of the editorial. The word 'issue' implies that it is a subject about which there is more than one point of view.

- Facts: the children should be clear about the facts relating to their chosen issue in order to determine points for and against.

- One side of the argument and The other side of the argument: the children should find at least two reasons to support the issue and two reasons against it. Remind them of the work they have done on 'for and against' format. (see Links to other units.) At this point you can explain that some editorials mention reasons which people with an opposing viewpoint may use but only if they can 'knock down' the argument or hold it up to ridicule. This is a sophisticated device which some children may be able to utilise, but, at this stage, the ability to put forward one opinion persuasively is sufficient.

- Editorial: the children should decide which side of the argument their editorial will support.

Be on hand to discuss the work in progress as some children will need guidance in their choice of issue, and prompting to find salient points on both sides of the argument. If possible, guide them to choose an issue currently related to school or their local community.

Session 2

Introduction
`10-15 min`

Before the children write up their editorials from their framework notes, recap on:

- the purpose of an editorial, i.e. to put forward one point of view in a persuasive style;
- the language, i.e. words and phrases to persuade the reader to adopt the same point of view as the writer;
- the balance between factual information and opinion, i.e. only the bare facts are used to introduce the issue. The bulk of an editorial is opinion.

Writing an editorial
`30min`

The children should write their editorial as a first draft which they can model on the paragraph organisation of **Copymaster 25**. They should be given the opportunity to discuss it with you on an individual basis before writing or word processing a final draft.

Homework

The children can produce their final draft for homework. For those who have grasped the idea and completed a satisfactory editorial, they can plan and write an editorial which supports the proposed building of the supermarket near Howden.

The Howden Herald

30p   *Saturday, 25th May*

Will supermarket starve local shops?

A national grocery chain has been granted planning permission to build a supermarket on the edge of Howden. The proposed site is to the north-east of the town, only ten minutes by car from the town centre.

Some of the local residents welcome the new supermarket. One man interviewed said, "It's about time we had a large shop where you can buy almost everything under one roof."

Not all the people are, however, in favour of this new development. A town centre shopkeeper felt that the new supermarket would mean that people would not come into the town to shop so often and her small grocery business would suffer.

Read the newspaper article carefully and make notes on the facts and opinions about the new supermarket.

FACTS

OPINIONS

Editorial

Is it time to stop making our town centres into ghost towns?

Our front page reports on the proposed building of a supermarket on the north-east edge of our town.

Surely it is time that local planners saw sense? Every time a supermarket or retail park is built near a town the shops in the town centre suffer. Every right-thinking person can see this.

Many of the shopkeepers along the High Street have been there for years, providing the people of Howden with a service which we seem to take for granted. Shopkeepers are voters too and it is about time that the local council listened seriously to their concerns.

If shops close, what happens to the people who do not have cars and cannot get to the supermarket? The real truth is that what may represent convenient shopping for some, will most definitely inconvenience others.

It is time to make a stand and stop bowing to the pressure put on local communities by the power and wealth of the multi-nationals.

The *Howden Herald* is heading a campaign to stop the supermarket being built. We need your signatures on our petition and your supporting views to print in our newspaper. Join us to stop the centre of Howden being turned into a ghost town!

Read the editorial carefully and make notes on:

a. the reasons the editor uses to persuade readers that the supermarket should not be built;

b. examples of persuasive words and phrases.

Editorial writing frame

Issue:

Facts:

One side of the argument:

The other side of the argument:

Editorial:

UNIT 3 | Advertisements

Learning targets

On completion of this unit the children should be able to:

1 ➤➤ read other examples, e.g. newspaper comment, headlines, adverts, fliers. Compare writing which informs and persuades, considering, e.g.
   - the deliberate use of ambiguity, half truth, bias;
   - how opinion can be disguised to seem like fact.

2 ➤➤ select and evaluate a range of texts, in print or other media, for persuasiveness, clarity, quality of information.

3 ➤➤ from reading, to collect and investigate use of persuasive devices: e.g. deliberate ambiguities, e.g. *'probably the best... in the world'*, *'known to cure all...'*; *'the professionals' choice'*.

Before you start

Resources for Session 1

Copymaster 27: Analysing copy
Copymaster 28: Advertising copy-writing frame

Links to other units

Learning Targets for Literacy: Non-Fiction Years 3 and 4, Year 4 Term 3 Unit 1, Year 4 Term 3 Unit 3

Assessment indicators

- Can the children analyse advertisements in terms of audience appeal and word play?
- Can they devise adverts using these techniques?

Teaching the session

Session 1 ① ② ③

Introduction 10-15 min

The children have had experience of advertising (see Links to other units) but it is worth revisiting as it provides the most immediate resource for looking at the language of persuasion in terms of careful and specific choices of words and phrases.

Begin by recapping on the main points of an advert:
- its purpose;
- its intended audience and how this affects the language, layout, visual image, etc.;
- the text used to inform and persuade.

The emphasis in this session is to look more closely at the text of adverts and how it:
- implies certain things about the reader who is 'persuaded';
- uses word play to create a memorable effect.

Explain to the children that the correct term for the text of an advert is 'copy'.

Analysing 'copy' 20 min

Give each group **Copymaster 27: Analysing copy**. In section A the children are investigating the audience in terms of who they think the advert is appealing to. Look at the first one as a class and ask what sort of person would be persuaded by an advert which had the copy 'The only car to be seen in'? It may help to give choices, e.g.
- someone who is not interested in cars;
- someone who sees a car as a functional vehicle to get them from A to B;
- someone who is very interested in cars and likes to drive the best/latest model.

In section B, the advertising copy in each case is using word play. Look at the first one as a class and ask:

What is clever about the choice of words?

You can help by making a diagrammatic connection, i.e.

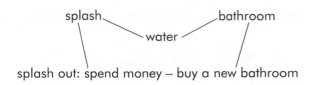

splash.............................bathroom
water

splash out: spend money – buy a new bathroom

The children are looking for connections in this way. Do they think the copy would have the same effect if it said 'Spend some money on a new bathroom'?

The children should work through section A making notes on audience appeal, and section B making notes on word play.

Summary 　　　　　　　　　　|10–15 min|

▦ Compare the children's findings through class discussion.

Section A
Obviously there are no definitive answers but the children should have notes along these lines:

- 'Give your kids the best start to the day': appealing to a parent's sense of wanting the best for their children
  What do the children think is being advertised? (breakfast cereal/fruit juice)

- 'You won't find a lower price': someone who is looking for a bargain.
  Do the advertisers expect everyone to actually look for a lower price?

- 'Latest technology at the lowest price': someone who always has to have the most modern equipment and who likes to think that they have got a bargain.
  What do the children think is being advertised? (computer/mobile phone, etc.)

- 'The sale of the century': someone who is looking for a bargain and is persuaded by exaggerated claims.
  Introduce the children to the term 'hyperbole' which means great exaggeration and is often used in advertising copy.

- 'If you want the best': someone who likes to think that only the best is good enough for them.

Discuss this type of advertising tactic with regard to designer labels on sportswear.

- 'The professionals' choice': someone who likes to think they are an expert or someone who believes that if professionals use the item then it must be good.
  What do the children think is being advertised? (possibly sports equipment) Discuss with the children that if a professional golfer, tennis player, footballer, etc. wears or uses a brand name, do they do so because it is the best or because they are being paid to advertise that brand?

- 'For people with good taste': someone who thinks that having the item is a sign of good taste.
  Do the children agree or do they think people are being hoodwinked?

Section B
- Purrfect food for your cat: purr – cat – perfect
- Isn't it time for a new watch?: watch – telling time – time for
- Get stuck into the World Wide Web: web – fly 'gets stuck' – get stuck into = get involved with/ become expert at

Writing advertising copy 　　|20–30min|

👤👥 The children can use **Copymaster 28: Advertising copy-writing frame** to support them in planning and drafting an advertisement. Obviously they need to use visual images but the copymaster concentrates their attention initially on the 'copy' needed for the advert.

The children should:
1 complete the copymaster and discuss it with you.
2 draft the layout of the advert, i.e. where copy and visuals will go.
3 produce a final draft of the advert, word processing the copy and sticking it in place where possible.

Homework

The children can look for adverts with interesting copy in newspapers and magazines. These can be mounted and displayed alongside their own work.

27 | Analysing copy

Section A

What sort of person would be persuaded by these?

THE ONLY CAR TO BE SEEN IN!

Give your kids the best start to the day.

The sale of the century

You won't find a lower price!

Latest technology at the lowest price

For people with good taste

If you want the best...

The professionals' choice

Section B

What 'word play' can you find in this copy?

1   Splash out on a new bathroom

2   Purrfect food for your cat

3   Isn't it time for a new watch?

4   Get stuck into the World Wide Web!

Advertising copy-writing frame

What is being advertised?

What sort of person do you want your advert to appeal to?

Possible words and phrases you might use in your advertisement.

Can you use any of your words or phrases for 'word play'?

Final copy for your advertisement.

UNIT 4 | Debates

Learning target

On completion of this unit the children should be able to:

1 ➤➤ construct an argument in note form or full text to persuade others of a point of view and:
- present the case to the class or a group;
- evaluate its effectiveness.

Before you start

Resources for Session 1

Copymaster 29: Planning an argument

Resources for Session 2

Copymaster 30: A balloon debate

Links to other units

Learning Targets for Literacy: Non-Fiction Years 3 *and* 4 Year 3 Term 2 Unit 3, Year 4 Term 3 Unit 2, Year 4 Term 3 Unit 1

Assessment indicators

Can the children make notes on a particular point of view?

Can they present their point of view to the class in the form of a debate?

Teaching the sessions

Session 1 ①

Introduction 20min

Begin by asking the children what they have learned about persuasive writing. Explain that there is a formal structure for putting across a point of view orally which is called debating. Some of the children may have had experience of taking part in a debate either as a speaker or in the audience and can assist you in outlining how a debate works.

Ensure that the children understand the following debating rules by using a role play situation:

- a debate has a specific subject called the 'motion'. For example:
  'This house believes that spending money on the space programme while people in the world are starving is wrong and should be stopped';
- there are two speakers in a debate – one to propose the motion, i.e. speak in favour of it, and one to oppose the motion, i.e. speak against it;
- the person speaking for the motion is the proposer;
- the person speaking against the motion is the opposer;

- The order of a debate is:
  proposer puts forward his or her point of view
  opposer puts forward his or her point of view
  the audience asks questions
  the proposer sums up
  the opposer sums up
  the audience votes.

The speakers in a debate must:
- know any relevant facts;
- support their point of view with evidence;
- have thought about what the other side may say and 'knock down' these arguments.

Preparing to debate 20min

Put the children into groups and give each pair of groups a motion, e.g.

This house believes that:
- it is wrong to keep animals in zoos;
- school should finish at 1 o'clock;
- school uniform should not be compulsory;
- fertilisers should not be used on crops;
- children should be able to go to bed at whatever time they like.

Both groups in each pair should use **Copymaster 29: Planning an argument** to structure the points they will raise in favour and in opposition of the motion, depending upon their standpoint.

Although many debating topics require research, the suggested topics rely mainly on the children's knowledge and experience in order to focus the work on the debate itself. There is, however, a section for 'facts' on the copymaster. If the motion is 'This house believes that school should finish at 1 o'clock' then the 'facts' are:

- school begins at 9 o'clock;
- school finishes at 3 o'clock;
- we spend six hours in school;

rather than statistical facts found through research.

Be on hand to help the children marshal their facts, plan their arguments and foresee and counter any arguments the opposition may put forward.

Summary 10-15 min

This can be a class discussion about the 'for' and 'against' arguments the children have come up with but, if at all possible, set some time aside over a week or fortnight for the actual debates to take place. Each group should choose one of their number to be the speaker and the rest of the group can watch but not participate in that debate.

Session 2 ❶

Introduction 10-15 min

Another form of debating which the children will enjoy is a balloon debate. Explain to the children that this consists of four famous people being in a hot air balloon. The balloon is rapidly losing height and three of them have to jump. They each have a turn to persuade the audience that they should be the one to stay in the balloon by:

- relating all the valuable things they have done in their life;
- giving reasons why each of the other three is not worth saving.

As in the more formal type of debate, the audience has an opportunity to ask questions. They then vote for the speaker they have found the most convincing.

A balloon debate 20 min

Copymaster 30: A balloon debate will support the children in planning what they will say in the debate. In choosing who is in the balloon to begin with, select historical figures with whom the children are familiar or characters from the class reader.

Summary 10-15 min

This can be a class discussion about the 'for' and 'against' arguments the children have come up with but, if at all possible, set some time aside over a week or fortnight for the actual debates to take place. Each group should choose one of their number to be the speaker and the rest of the group can watch but not participate in that debate.

Planning an argument

The motion:

Are you: proposing? ▢   opposing? ▢

What facts do you need?

What arguments will you use?

What arguments could the other side use?

How can you 'knock down' these arguments?

A balloon debate

Who are you?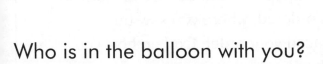

Who is in the balloon with you?

Why should you be saved?

Why should the others
be thrown out?

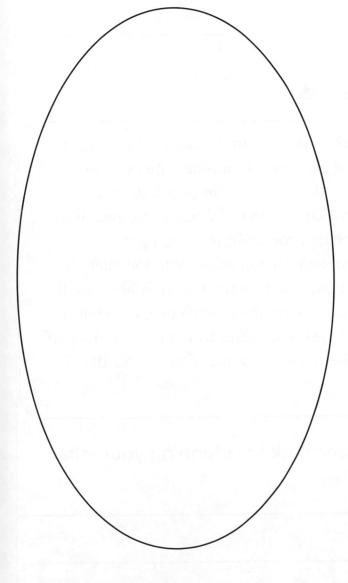

1

2

3

Writing composition
Letters

Section A: letters of complaint

You ordered a CD from a magazine advertisement seven weeks ago. The advertisement promised delivery within 28 days but it still hasn't arrived. Write to the company to complain about their slow service. Include in the letter the details of the CD you ordered, where you saw the advertisement and the date you placed your order. Explain how you would like the situation to be resolved.

Use Copymaster 19 as a framework for planning your letter.

Notes _____

_____

Section B: letters to persuade

The town council wants to knock down your local play area to build a new road. They plan to move the play area to another site but you will have to cross the new road to get there. Explain in your letter how important the play area is to your community and how dangerous it will be for small children to cross the new road. Put forward your suggestions for resolving the problem. One possible solution might be to build the new road on the site intended for the new play area. Or, if the new road is built, to put a crossing on the road to help the children get to the new play area safely. Finish your letter by explaining which of your suggestions you think will be the best course of action for the council to take.

Use Copymaster 23 as a framework for planning your letter.

Notes _____

_____

Writing composition
Editorials

Imagine you are the editor of a local newspaper and choose **one** of the following on which to write an editorial:

In your area, the morning post has been arriving later and later. There are just too many houses for one postman to deliver to.

Letters of complaint have been received by your newspaper because the post office will not do anything about the situation.

Write an editorial which supports the idea that more postmen should be employed to deliver the post in your area.

The main street in your small town is always filled with large lorries which have to pass through the town to get to the motorway.

The people of the town have been campaigning for a by-pass to be built but with no success.

Write an editorial supporting the idea that a by-pass should be built.

Use Copymaster 26 as a framework for planning your editorial.

YEAR 6 TERM 1

Focus

Year 6 Term 1 National Literacy non-fiction objectives cover biographical and autobiographical writing, journalistic style and revise the main elements of report writing.

Throughout the units the children are given the opportunity to analyse the new styles of non-fiction writing and revise report writing with the emphasis on using this skill in other curriculum areas.

The non-fiction objectives require emphasis on research and note-taking and you may find that more time has to be given to this than has been indicated. In essence, these tasks, as with many at this level, fall into the category of extended writing and, as such, should be continued outside of the designated literacy hour.

Content

Unit 1: Biography and autobiography
Unit 2: Journalistic writing
Unit 3: Report writing

Assessment

At the end of this section there are two copymasters to assess:

• Biography and autobiography

Copymaster 41 gives the children a choice of starting points for researching a famous person and writing either as a biographer or autobiographer. Copymaster 34, a planning sheet used in Unit 1, can be given to the children to support their research and note-taking.

• Journalistic writing

Copymaster 42 gives the children the basic facts of a scenario about which they must write two newspaper reports – one biased and the other balanced.

Copymaster 38, used in Unit 2, can be given to the children to support them in the planning stage.

Curriculum Planner
National Literacy Strategy Planner

This chart shows you how to find activities by unit to resource your term's requirements for text level work on non-fiction. The learning targets closely follow the structure of the non-fiction requirements for the term in the National Literacy Strategy document (page 51). A few of the requirements are not covered.

YEAR 6   Term 1

Range

Non-fiction

- autobiography and biography, diaries, journals, letters, anecdotes, records of observations, etc. which recount experiences and events;
- journalistic writing;
- non-chronological reports.

TEXT LEVEL WORK

COMPREHENSION AND COMPOSITION

Reading comprehension

Pupils should be taught:

11 to distinguish between biography and autobiography;
  - recognising the effect on the reader of the choice between first and third person;
  - distinguishing between fact, opinion and fiction;
  - distinguishing between implicit and explicit points of view and how these can differ; Unit 1

12 to comment critically on the language, style, success of examples of non-fiction such as periodicals, reviews, reports, leaflets; Unit 2

13 to secure understanding of the features of non-chronological reports:
  - introductions to orientate reader;
  - use of generalisations to categorise;
  - language to describe and differentiate;
  - impersonal language;
  - mostly present tense; Unit 3

Writing composition

14 to develop the skills of biographical and autobiographical writing in role, adopting distinctive voices, e.g. historical characters through, e.g.
  - preparing a CV;
  - composing a biographical account based on research;
  - describing a person from different perspectives, e.g. police description, school report, newspaper obituary; Unit 1

15 to develop a journalistic style through considering:
  - balanced and ethical reporting;
  - what is of public interest in events;
  - the interest of the reader;
  - selection and presentation of information; Unit 2

16 use the styles and conventions of journalism to report on, e.g. real or imagined events; Unit 2

17 to write non-chronological reports linked to other subjects; Unit 3

Biography and autobiography

Learning targets

On completion of this unit the children should be able to:

1 ➡➡➡ distinguish between biography and autobiography;
- recognising the effect on the reader of the choice between first and third person;
- distinguishing between fact, opinion and fiction;
- distinguishing between implicit and explicit points of view and how these can differ.

2 ➡➡➡ develop the skills of biographical and autobiographical writing in role, adopting distinctive voices, e.g. historical characters through, e.g.:
- preparing a c.v.;
- composing a biographical account based on research;
- describing a person from different perspectives, e.g. police description, school report, newspaper obituary.

Before you start

Resources for Session 1

Copymaster 33: Research
Copymaster 34: Biography – William Shakespeare

Resources for session 2

Copymaster 35: Autobiography – Roald Dahl

Links to other units

Learning Targets for Literacy: Fiction and Poetry Years 3 and 4 Year 3 Term 3 Unit 2

Assessment indicators

- Can the children differentiate between biography and autobiography?
- Can they distinguish fact from opinion/supposition?
- Can they research facts for a biographical account?
- Can they use an autobiographical style to write about incidents in their own lives?

Teaching the sessions

Session 1 ❶ ❷

Introduction [15-20 min]

▓ Session 1 will concentrate on biographies. Explain to the children that a biography is an account of a person's life written by someone else, i.e. in the third person. This type of writer is called a biographer. One of the earliest biographers we know of is a man called Plutarch who wrote biographies of famous Greeks and Romans around AD 100.

If the person being written about is still alive, the biographer will try to talk to that person and get a first hand account of events in his or her life. A good biographer should also talk to other people to get a balanced view of what they are writing about.

Biographies are often written about people after they have died. Sometimes the family will let the biographer read the person's letters and diaries, and people will feel able to speak more freely about someone who is no longer living.

Discuss with the children what they think a good biography should include so the reader has a balanced and detailed account of the person's life, e.g.

• the facts about his or her life;
• his or her personality;
• how what he or she did affected others;
• a balanced point of view looking at as much evidence as possible;
• gossip – can be included but should not lead the reader to believe that this is fact.

Have the children read any biographies?

Looking at a biography   20–30min

Give each group **Copymaster 34: Biography – William Shakespeare**. Scholarship about the bard is constantly uncovering more details of his life and work and this can form the basis of a discussion with the children, i.e. is there any need to continue to write biographies of famous, long-dead people if one has already been written?

The children should discuss in groups:

• the opening paragraph;
• the facts they learn about Shakespeare – what words and phrases does the writer use so that the reader knows these are the facts?
• the opinions/suppositions about his life – what words and phrases does the writer use so the reader knows these are not hard facts?
• the sequence of the information.

The children can use different coloured highlighters to mark 'facts' and 'opinions/suppositions' on the copymaster.

Summary   15–20min

 Discuss the extract with the children.

The opening

• It does not begin in a predictable way, i.e. 'William Shakespeare was born in Stratford-upon-Avon on…etc.';
• It relates the life of this man who lived over 400 years ago to the present day;
• It captures the reader's interest.

The facts

• Compile a list on the board of the 'facts' in the extract based on suggestions from the children;
• Look at words/phrases used to signal the facts, e.g.
  'We do know, however…'
  'he must have…'
  'We can be sure…'
  'We do know for certain…'

The opinions/suppositions

• Compile a list on the board of opinions/suppositions in the extract based on suggestions from the children;

• Look at words/phrases used to signal opinion/supposition, e.g.
  'Nobody really knows…'
  'We believe…'
  'Some writers say…'
  'It may have been so…'
  'Many people think…'
  'Some people say…'

The sequence

• The children will see that the biographical detail is moving from when Shakespeare was born, in chronological order through his life. Explain that this is the most common way of writing a biography, but some biographers do begin in the middle or even at the end of someone's life and track back to earlier events.

Do the children think it would be easier to write a biography of a person who is still alive or one who is dead?

Research   30min

Copymaster 33: Research will support the children in researching an historical character on which to base a short biographical account, or, if you feel it is more appropriate, the children can interview each other. In both cases, the element of supposition will be difficult. If you wish the children to include this element in their writing, then suggest that they make up a 'famous person' about whom some facts are known and others can only be guessed at. They can model their biography on **Copymaster 34**, using words and phrases picked out in the summary discussion.

Homework

The children can complete their short biographies for homework.

Session 2

Introduction   10–15 min

 Session 2 will concentrate on autobiographies. Explain to the children that an autobiography is a person's account of his or her own life and is therefore written in the first person. The word 'autobiography' is made up of three Greek words:
  auto – self
  bios – life
  graphos – writing

Discuss with the children:

• why they think someone might choose to write a book about their own life;
• in what ways an autobiography might differ from a biography?

Have the children read any autobiographies?

Autobiography $\boxed{\text{20-30min}}$

♣ Give each group **Copymaster 35: Autobiography – Roald Dahl.** As with Copymaster 34, the children should look for the facts in the extract but they should also look for things which could not have been included if this was a biographical account.

Explain that this is an extract from the second part of Dahl's autobiography. The fist volume *Boy* told of his early years and schooling. This volume entitled *Going Solo* begins with his voyage out to East Africa for his first job. The extract is a memorable incident in Tanganyika.

Summary $\boxed{\text{20min}}$

▦ Discuss the children's reaction to the extract. In what ways do they think it differs from the biographical extract they read? For example:

- first person account;
- more detail as the writer was actually there;
- direct speech – unlikely that a biographer can include exactly what was said;
- a real sense of knowing how the writer was feeling.

Investigate the opening of the chapter. Why do the children think that Dahl did not start the chapter 'One Sunday evening I was invited…'?

Point out to the children that while Roald Dahl is writing an autobiography about this event, he is also including short biographical details about the other people, e.g.

> Mr Fuller: 'He was completely cool and unruffled'
> The children: 'They didn't seem to be particularly alarmed'

He cannot tell the reader how Mr Fuller and the children were feeling 'inside'. He can only describe how they appeared to be feeling.

Writing an autobiography $\boxed{\text{30min}}$

👤 The children can undertake autobiographical writing in a number of ways:

- a straightforward time line about themselves from birth to the present day;
- a c.v. which details their achievements and interests;
- an account of an interesting/exciting event in their life.

The last option is by far the most interesting and will give the children the opportunity to write at length in the first person. Encourage the children to work in draft form at this stage.

Homework

The children can write or word process a neat copy of their work which can then be displayed.

I am writing a short
biography about:

Dates: Born [   ] Died [   ]

Famous for:

Main events in his or her life:

Opinions/suppositions:

Biography – William Shakespeare

Almost in the centre of England stands the old town of Stratford-upon-Avon. It is a beautiful old-world town which has thousands of visitors every year. They come from the four corners of the world to visit the birthplace of the most famous poet of all time, William Shakespeare. Stratford-upon-Avon is always considered Shakespeare's town, although his great work was done in London, but there is no doubt that much of his inspiration came from the wonderful country near his home.

If you visit Stratford you will find many reminders of Shakespeare and his times. There is the house where he was born, the Grammar School which he attended, and the old farmhouse in a neighbouring village where his wife lived. He was born on 23rd April, 1564, to parents who, whilst not very rich, were in comfortable circumstances. His father dealt in meat, skins and similar products, and when he was old enough William was sent to Stratford Grammar School. His schoolmaster, Master Roche, believed that to spare the rod was to spoil the child, and we can be sure school was not a very pleasant place. Lessons commenced at six o'clock

in the morning, and with half an hour's interval for breakfast they continued until half-past eleven. Afternoon school started at one o'clock, and continued until half past five, with only one half-hour's interval. At lunch William would wait on his parents at table, and when they had finished he would start. He would always address his father as 'sir'.

Why did Shakespeare leave Stratford?

At thirteen years of age Shakespeare had to leave the Grammar School, as his father's business had declined and he had become a poor man. Nobody really knows what Shakespeare did in the next five years. We do know, however, that when he was eighteen he married Anne Hathaway, a lady eight years his

Biography – William Shakespeare
(cont.)

senior. We believe the marriage was not very successful, and when Shakespeare was twenty-one we hear of him going up to London. Some writers say that he left Stratford in a hurry as he had got into trouble poaching deer on the estate of Sir Thomas Lucy, at Charlecote, three miles out of Stratford. It may have been so, but it was a common practice of bright young men in those days to go up to London to seek their fortunes.

Of his first eight years in London, nothing is known. Many people think he must have travelled abroad, so great is the knowledge of foreign customs and characters shown in his plays. Whatever he did, he must have mixed with 'all sorts and conditions of men' and that is a fine education for an alert mind. We can be sure he had visited both the London theatres, the Curtain in Moor Fields and the Theatre in Shoreditch. Both theatres were outside London in those days, and gentlemen rode on their horses to either of them. Some people say that Shakespeare held the gentlemen's horses at one time. We do know for certain, however, that he soon obtained work in the theatre.

Later he became an actor, and afterwards was employed altering plays and making them suitable for stage production. It is not a long step from adapting plays to writing plays, and when he was twenty-seven Shakespeare wrote his first play, *Love's Labour's Lost*.

from *A Pageant of History* Collins 1966

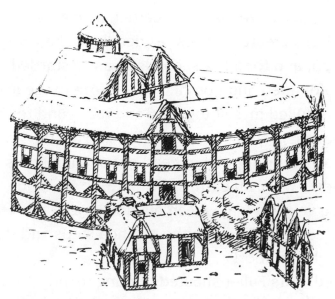

Shakespeare's Globe Theatre

Autobiography – Roald Dahl

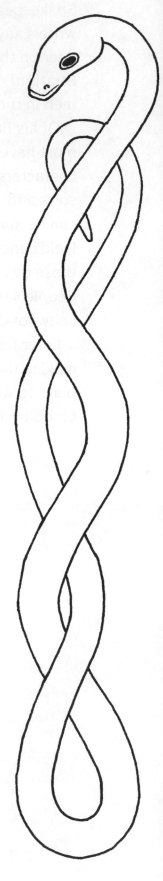

The Green Mamba

Oh, those snakes! How I hated them! They were the only fearful thing about Tanganyika, and a newcomer very quickly learnt to identify most of them and to know which were deadly and which were simply poisonous. The killers, apart from the black mambas, were the green mambas, the cobras and the tiny little puff adders that looked very much like small sticks lying motionless in the middle of a dusty path, and so easy to step on.

One Sunday evening I was invited to go and have a sundowner at the house of an Englishman called Fuller who worked in the Customs office in Dar es Salaam. He lived with his wife and two small children in a plain white wooden house that stood alone some way back from the road in a rough grassy piece of ground with coconut trees scattered about. I was walking across the grass towards the house and was about twenty yards away when I saw a large green snake go gliding straight up the veranda steps of Fuller's house and in through the open front door. The brilliant yellowy-green skin and its great size made me certain it was a green mamba, a creature almost as deadly as the black mamba, and for a few seconds I was so startled and dumbfounded and horrified that I froze to the spot. Then I pulled myself together and ran round to the back of the house shouting, 'Mr Fuller! Mr Fuller!'

Mrs Fuller popped her head out of an upstairs window. 'What on earth's the matter?' she said.

'You've got a large green mamba in your front room!' I shouted. 'I saw it go up the veranda steps and right in through the door!'

'Fred!' Mrs Fuller shouted, turning round. 'Fred! Come here!'

Freddy Fuller's round red face appeared at the window beside his wife. 'What's up?' he asked.

'There's a green mamba in your living room!' I shouted.

Autobiography – Roald Dahl (cont.)

Without hesitation and without wasting time with more questions, he said to me, 'Stay there. I'm going to lower the children down to you one at a time.' He was completely cool and unruffled. He didn't even raise his voice.

A small girl was lowered down to me by her wrists and I was able to catch her easily by the legs. Then came a small boy. Then Freddy Fuller lowered his wife and I caught her by the waist and put her on the ground. Then came Fuller himself. He hung by his hands from the window-sill and when he let go he landed neatly on his two feet.

We stood in a little group on the grass at the back of the house and I told Fuller exactly what I had seen.

The mother was holding the two children by the hand, one on each side of her. They didn't seem to be particularly alarmed.

'What happens now?' I asked.

'Go down the road, all of you,' Fuller said. 'I'm off to fetch the snake-man.' He trotted away and got into his small ancient black car and drove off. Mrs Fuller and the two small children and I went down to the road and sat in the shade of a large mango tree.

'Who is this snake-man?' I asked Mrs Fuller.

'He is an old Englishman who has been out here for years,' Mrs Fuller said. 'He actually *likes* snakes. He understands them and never kills them. He catches them and sells them to zoos and laboratories all over the world. Every native for miles around knows about him and whenever one of them sees a snake, he marks its hiding place and runs, often for great distances, to tell the snake-man…

From *Going Solo* by Roald Dahl

Journalistic writing

Learning targets

On completion of this unit the children should be able to:

1 ➡➡ develop a journalistic style through considering:
- balanced and ethical reporting;
- what is of public interest in events;
- interest of the reader;
- selection and presentation of information.

2 ➡➡ use the styles and conventions of journalism to report on, e.g. real or imagined events.

Before you start

Resources for Session 1

Copymaster 36: Better team beaten
Copymaster 37: Sides separated by lone goal
Copymaster 38: Balanced reporting

Links to other units

Learning Targets for Literacy: Non-Fiction Years 3 and 4 Year 3 Term 3 Unit 2, Year 4 Term 1 Unit 2, Year 4 Term 3 Unit 3
Learning Targets for Literacy: Non-Fiction Years 5 and 6 Year 5 Term 3 Unit 2

Assessment indicators

- Can the children recognise the viewpoint from which a newspaper report is written?
- Can they judge when a newspaper report is balanced?
- Can they write both biased and balanced newspaper reports?

Teaching the session

Session 1 ① ②

Introduction `15-20 min`

▓ Begin by recapping on the various items found in newspapers which the children have worked on, i.e. reports, fact and opinion, editorials and advertisements (see Links to other units).

Explain that you are going to look at newspaper reports again, concentrating on how balanced and detailed the report is, as opposed to a one sided account where the writer is only presenting his or her interpretation of events, omitting details which would not support his or her particular standpoint.

This is a good opportunity to discuss what the children think is the purpose of a newspaper report. Do they think it should be written to:

- persuade the reader to agree with the writer's viewpoint;
- present the facts with no comment;

- present the facts and comment on the variety of ways in which the facts can be interpreted, i.e. give equal weight to both sides of an issue?

Hopefully the children will draw on their knowledge of editorials to see that different articles in a newspaper can have different functions, but that, in the main, a newspaper should give an unbiased account of the news.

Did they watch the same match? `20-25 min`

 Give each group **Copymaster 36: Better team beaten**, and **Copymaster 37: Sides separated by lone goal**. Explain to the children that they are both accounts of the same football match and ask them to discuss which report they judge to be more balanced and why? They should make notes on:

- the facts in each report;
- any facts that are contradictory;
- how the writer interprets/chooses to present those facts.

Summary

 Base a class discussion on how the children have analysed the two reports.

Better team beaten

The writer is obviously a Stanton Wanderers supporter and has chosen to report that the goal was scored against the run of play, i.e. the 'luckiest of goals'. His report contains a glaring contradiction; it states that Biggin United were hardly in the game and then a few lines later reports that Stanton's defenders cleared the ball 'expertly when danger threatened'. He claims the referee was not paying enough attention and that this contributed to Stanton's defeat.

His account of how the goal was scored gives the reader the impression that it was due to an uneven pitch and not to any skill of the Biggin player.

Teams Separated by Lone Goal

This report is balanced and gives details which the reader would be interested in, i.e. the relegation battle.

His account gives the reader the impression that both teams played well and that the result could have gone either way.

He picks out a Stanton player who made some careless passes and a Biggin player who almost scored an own goal.

The referee saw what the other reporter claimed he had missed and waved play on.

His account of the goal allows the goal scorer to take some credit for scoring it.

Discuss which report the children think is most valuable to the reader.

Balanced or Biased

 The children can follow up their analysis of the football reports with two writing activities:

1   Based on what they know of the Stanton v Biggin football match, the children should write a third report as if they were a reporter who supported Biggin United. This should be deliberately biased to show that Biggin should have won.

2   Choose an issue which is relevant to the children and ask them to plan and write a balanced newspaper report about it. **Copymaster 38: Balanced reporting** will help them to plan and organise their work.

The Town Crier

25p   Saturday 21st February

Better Team Beaten

Stanton Wanderers 0   Biggin United 1

by Alex Boots

Saturday's football match at Stanton's ground saw the better side beaten by a fluke goal in the 77th minute.

Up until that luckiest of goals, Stanton Wanderers were by far the better side. They had the ball most of the time, hardly allowing Biggin United into the game.

Stanton's midfield players passed superbly, especially Ian Wrong who controlled the match from his position as centre forward.

Carter and Maine, Stanton's defenders were solid at the back, clearing the ball expertly when danger threatened.

Biggin United had one good move, but even this began from what was obviously a foul tackle on Stanton's left winger, Brian Riggs. Having won the ball illegally when the referee was obviously looking the other way, Coalman raced down the wing and made a lucky pass to the centre forward, Bates.

Bates, for a moment looking as if he had never seen a football before, suddenly woke up, stumbled forward and aimed a half-hearted kick towards the goal.

Stanton's goalkeeper did a superb dive to block the ball but it hit uneven turf and bounced over his outstretched hands to make it 1–0 to Biggin United.

Not a fair goal and not a fair result.

Sports Review

28p   Saturday 21st February

Sides Separated By Lone Goal

Stanton Wanderers 0   Biggin United 1

by Alan Fare

An important match for Stanton Wanderers and Biggin United, both in the relegation zone of Division 2, took place at the Stanton ground on Saturday.

Both teams badly needed the points to avoid playing 3rd Division football next season. It was only a well taken goal in the 77th minute that divided them as both played with determination and to the highest standard.

Play in the first half was fairly even with each side having long spells of possession. Both centre forwards, Stanton's Ian Wrong and United's Paul Peville, played strong, attacking football but the occasional careless pass from Brian Riggs allowed Biggin to have a few shots on target.

Carter and Maine, Stanton's backs, defended solidly. Biggin's defender, Jones, almost scored an own goal but was saved from embarrassment by the goalkeeper, Merrett.

The scores were 0–0 at half time but the second half was to tell a different story. Biggin United stepped up a gear and were constantly on the attack throughout the entire 45 minutes. They were eventually rewarded 13 minutes from the end by the only goal of the match.

Coalman went in hard to tackle Riggs and, although several Stanton players stopped to protest, the referee waved play on. Coalman was given acres of space by the motionless Stanton players to race down the wing and pass the ball to Bates, waiting on the 18 yard line. At first, it looked as if Bates wasn't sure what to do but the sprint forward and cleverly lofted shot which bounced over the goalkeeper, was masterly.

It was obvious a few minutes into the game that the sides were evenly matched and it was always on the cards that a single goal would decide the day.

Balanced reporting

The issue:

The main facts:

Other related facts which will interest the reader:

How the facts can be interpreted, i.e. points of view:

1

2

3

Report writing

Learning targets

1 ➤➤ secure understanding of the features of non-chronological reports;
- introductions to orientate reader;
- use of generalisations to categorise;
- language to describe and differentiate;
- impersonal language;
- mostly present tense.

2 ➤➤ write non-chronological reports linked to other subjects.

Before you start

Resources for Session 1

Copymaster 39: Italy
Copymaster 40: Report research

Links to other units

Learning Targets for Literacy: Non-Fiction Years 5 and 6 Year 5 Term 1 Unit 1, Year 5 Term 2 Unit 2

Assessment indicators

- Can the children research a topic from another curriculum area?

- Can they make notes and organise them into coherent paragraphs?
- Can they introduce the topic in a clear way to orientate the reader?
- Can they differentiate when to use the past and present tenses in report writing?
- Can they acknowledge their sources in the form of a bibliography?

Teaching the session

Session 1 ① ②

Introduction 15-20min

The children have had experience of writing various types of reports so this session is an opportunity for them to practise the skills of note-taking and acknowledging sources, as well as revising the elements of report-writing.

Discuss with the children what they understand by the term 'report' and ask for examples, e.g. newspaper report, report on a visit, event, etc. Explain that when they research a subject for topic work and then write up their notes they are, in fact, writing a report on information they have discovered.

Give each child **Copymaster 39: Italy** and explain that the writer was given the task of researching facts about Italy and that these are a set of notes the

writer has made using various information books.

Discuss with the children how they would use these notes to write a 'report' on Italy, considering:

- the function of the first paragraph, i.e. to orientate the reader;
- the organisation, i.e. grouping the notes together according to areas of information rather than writing what they found out in each book in turn;
- style, i.e. mostly present tense except when they are referring to a past event, e.g.

  Italy *is* a country in Southern Europe...

  The last emperor *ruled* in AD 476...

Organising notes for a report 20-30min

In groups the children should work out how they would organise the notes into a report. Using different coloured highlighters they should:

- highlight the notes from each information source which have a common theme;
- decide how many paragraphs are needed;
- order the paragraphs;
- write a brief introduction;
- compile a bibliography.

The notes should be grouped as follows:

- geography – situation, rivers, seas and islands;
- history – rule from Rome, invasions, emperor, Empire and World War I;
- economy – crops, manufactured goods and exports;
- tourism – sites visited.

Summary

 Discuss how the groups have organised the notes, compiled the bibliography and introduced the report. Ask the children which paragraphs of the report will be written in the present tense and which in the past.

Researching and writing ⏱ 30 min

👤 The children can follow up this analysis of the notes with a choice of the following writing activities, or you may have a subject relevant to current topic work on which to base this type of writing:

1 Using the notes on Italy as the basis of their report the children can do further research on Italy to gather more information, making a note of the books they consult. These notes should be integrated into the paragraphs they have already established, or new paragraphs can be added if appropriate, e.g. language, Italian artists, etc.

2 Using **Copymaster 40: Report research**, the children can choose a different country to research. Once the notes have been compiled they should organise them in the same way as the notes on Italy, i.e. grouping notes for paragraphing, ordering the paragraphs, making notes for the introduction and compiling the bibliography.

Once you have checked that the notes have been coherently grouped and ordered, the children should then write their report.

situated in southern Europe

main rivers – Po, Tiber, Arno, Adige

275 BC most of country ruled from Rome

(*A short history of Italy*, M. Frome)

two main offshore islands – Sicily/Sardinia

main crops – wheat/maize

after 4th century AD invaded by barbarian tribes, e.g. Visigoths/Vandals

principal manufactured goods – textiles/chemicals

(*Worldwide Encyclopaedia*)

main crops – olives/grapes/wheat

tourist industry important – visitors to Vatican, Colosseum, etc.

last Roman emperor – AD 476

World War 1 – Italy on Allies' side

(*Italy: Land of wine and sunshine* by A. Vine)

seas on three sides: east – Adriatic sea

west – Tyrrhenian sea

south – Ionian

main exports – chemicals, motor vehicles, fruit, vegetables, clothes

Roman Empire: 27 BC – AD 476

Many visitors to Pantheon

(*Italy* by C. Shore)

Report subject:

Source 1   book/magazine/CD-ROM

Title: Author:
Notes:

Source 2   book/magazine/CD-ROM

Title: Author:
Notes:

Source 3   book/magazine/CD-ROM

Title: Author:
Notes:

Source 4   book/magazine/CD-ROM

Title: Author:
Notes:

Writing composition
Biography and autobiography

Choose **one** of the following:

> a famous historical person

> a famous person alive today

1 Research the person you have chosen, concentrating on:
   • why he or she is famous;
   • one important event in his or her life.

2 Decide if:
   • you are going to be a biographer and write in the third person;
   • you are going to imagine that you are writing about yourself and write an autobiography in the first person.

Remember:

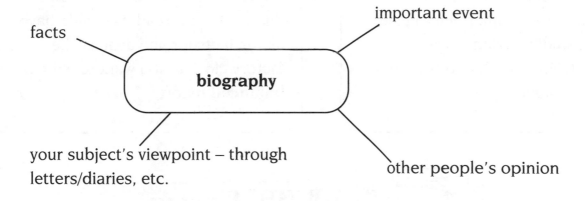

facts — **biography** — important event

your subject's viewpoint – through letters/diaries, etc.

other people's opinion

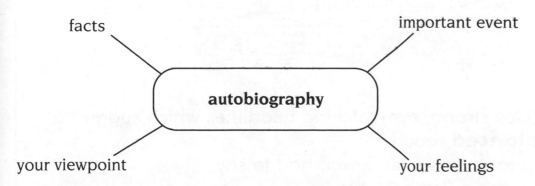

facts — **autobiography** — important event

your viewpoint

your feelings

Writing composition
Journalistic writing

Write **two** newspaper reports on the following:

> The issue:
> A factory in your town is situated near a river. For many years it has been discharging chemicals into the river and has refused to do anything about it, although fish and other wildlife are dying. The Town Council has decided to shut the factory down and many people will lose their jobs.

The newspaper reports

Write a newspaper report about the factory closure as a journalist for the *Daily News*. Some of your relatives work in the factory and will lose their jobs. You do not think polluting the river and wildlife dying is very important. You are **biased** towards the factory staying open.

Write a newspaper report about the factory closure as a journalist for the *Herald*.
You can see both points of view and think that your readers should have all the facts for and against the factory closing. You want to write a **balanced** report.

Remember:
- Give your articles strong, eye-catching headlines which suggest a **biased** or **balanced** report.
- Include what people you interviewed had to say.

YEAR 6 TERM 2

Focus

Year 6 Term 2 National Literacy non-fiction objectives cover discussion texts and the use of 'official' language.

Throughout the units the children are given the opportunity to analyse and write texts which are discursive in style, building on earlier work on persuasive language. Looking at official language is always difficult because of the alien contexts in which it usually occurs, so the emphasis in Unit 2 is on the necessity of precise language in given contexts.

Content

Unit 1: Discussion texts
Unit 2: Formal writing

Assessment

At the end of this section copymaster 48 can be used to assess discursive writing.

The children are given a variety of starting points from which to choose. Copymaster 44 can be used in the assessment as an aid to planning.

Curriculum Planner
National Literacy Strategy Planner

This chart shows you how to find activities by unit to resource your term's requirements for text level work on non-fiction. The learning targets closely follow the structure of the non-fiction requirements for the term in the National Literacy Strategy document (page 53). A few of the requirements are not covered.

YEAR 6 Term 2

Range

Non-fiction

- discussion texts: texts which set out, balance and evaluate different points of view, e.g. pros and cons of a course of action, moral issue, policy, etc.
- formal writing, notices, public and information documents.

TEXT LEVEL WORK

COMPREHENSION AND COMPOSITION

Reading comprehension

Pupils should be taught:

15 to recognise how arguments are constructed to be effective, through, e.g.:
- the expression, sequence and linking of points;
- the provision of persuasive examples, illustrations and evidence;
- pre-empting or answering potential objections;
- appealing to the known views and feelings of the audience; Unit 1

16 to identify the features of balanced written arguments which, e.g.:
- summarise different sides of an argument;
- clarify the strengths and weaknesses of different positions;
- signal personal opinion clearly; Unit 1

17 to read and understand examples of official language and its characteristic features, e.g. through discussing consumer information, legal documents, layouts, use of footnotes, instructions, parentheses, headings, appendices and asterisks; Unit 2

Writing composition

Pupils should be taught:

19 to write a balanced report of a controversial issue:
- summarising fairly the competing views;
- analysing strengths and weaknesses of different positions; Unit 1

20 to discuss the way standard English varies in different contexts, e.g. why legal language is necessarily highly formalised, why questionnaires must be specific; Unit 2

Discussion texts

Learning targets

On completion of this unit the children should be able to:

1 ➤➤ recognise how arguments are constructed to be effective, through, e.g.:
- the expression, sequence and linking of points;
- the provision of persuasive examples, illustrations and evidence;
- pre-empting or answering potential objections;
- appealing to the known views and feelings of the audience.

2 ➤➤ identify the features of balanced written arguments which, e.g.:
- summarise different sides of an argument;
- clarify the strengths and weaknesses of different positions;
- signal personal opinion clearly.

3 ➤➤ write a balanced report of a controversial issue:
- summarising fairly the competing views;
- analysing strengths and weaknesses of different positions.

Before you start

Resources for Session 1

Copymaster 43: Looking at discursive writing
Copymaster 44: Does the Loch Ness Monster really exist?

Links to other units

Learning Targets for Literacy: Non-Fiction Years 3 and 4 Year 3 Term 2 Unit 3, Year 4 Term 3 Unit 1, Year 4 Term 3 Unit 2
Learning Targets for Literacy: Non-fiction Years 5 and 6 Year 5 Term 3 Unit 4

Assessment indicators

- Can the children analyse a piece of discursive writing to formulate a model for their own writing?
- Can they present, in writing, both sides of an issue and reach a conclusion?

Teaching the session

Session 1 ➀ ➁ ➂

Introduction [10-15 min]

▦ The children have worked on persuasive writing in earlier units on presenting an argument and debates (see Links to other units). Explain to the children that the emphasis in this unit is to construct a piece of writing which:
- introduces the issue;
- presents one side of an argument;
- presents the other side of the argument;
- comes to a conclusion.

That is not to say that the writer cannot have strong views about which side of the argument he or she thinks carries more weight. For an argument to be effective the writer must look at both sides, showing the reader that one side is weaker through reasoned argument rather than just being dismissive. Equally, the writer may not be able to come to a definite conclusion and essentially, sums up the evidence and leaves it to the reader to make his or her own decision.

The Loch Ness Monster [20-30 min]

⚏ Give each group **Copymaster 44: Does the Loch Ness Monster really exist?**, which is a model for discursive writing, and **Copymaster 43: Looking at discursive writing**, on which they can make their notes. Explain that they must look at each paragraph, summarise the evidence and then decide if this evidence supports the existence of the monster or refutes it, i.e. does not support the existence of the monster.

Summary 15-20min

Base a class discussion on the children's findings which should be along these lines:

Introductory paragraph: orientates the reader and presents the subject to be discussed in the essay

Paragraph 2: first sighting of monster – support

Paragraph 3: photographic evidence – support

Paragraph 4: photographic evidence from scientists – support

Paragraph 4: other interpretations of photographic evidence – refute

Paragraph 5: unsuccessful scientific research – refute

Concluding paragraph: brief summary of evidence both for and against – undecided

From the children's analysis, they should see a basic model for discursive writing, i.e.

introduction – paragraph to support – paragraph to support – paragraph to refute – paragraph to refute – conclusion

Obviously, there can be more or less paragraphs, or evidence can be written and refuted in the same paragraph. This, however, is a simple model to help children deal with a sophisticated writing activity.

Discursive writing 30min

Give the children the following titles to choose from:

• Should corporal punishment be allowed in school?
• Is there life on other planets?
• Is playing computer games a waste of time?
• Should PE in school be a matter of choice?

Copymaster 43 can be used to help the children plan their work.

If you feel that a whole class discussion would be appropriate, choose one of the titles which all the children will write about. Discuss with the class what evidence they could put forward for supporting and what evidence for refuting. Allow them to make notes while the discussion is in progress.

Check each child's plan before they begin to draft the essay.

Introductory paragraph

What do you think the purpose of the introductory paragraph is?

_____

_____

Paragraph 2   support [   ]   refute [   ]

Summarise the evidence in one sentence.

_____

_____

Paragraph 3   support [   ]   refute [   ]

Summarise the evidence in one sentence.

_____

_____

Paragraph 4   support [   ]   refute [   ]

Summarise the evidence in one sentence.

_____

_____

Paragraph 5   support [   ]   refute [   ]

Summarise the evidence in one sentence.

_____

_____

Paragraph 6   support [   ]   refute [   ]

Summarise the evidence in one sentence.

_____

_____

Concluding paragraph

What conclusion is reached?

   for [   ]   against [   ]   undecided [   ]

Does the Loch Ness Monster really exist?

The Loch Ness Monster is a subject which has fascinated people from the first supposed sighting in AD 565 to the present day. Many people are convinced the monster exists in the deep water of the Scottish loch, while others are equally sure that it is just a figment of the imagination.

The first sighting of the Loch Ness Monster was some 1400 years ago by St Columba. One of St Columba's followers was swimming across the loch to fetch a boat when, suddenly, the monster appeared at the surface. St Columba made the sign of the cross and said, 'Think not to go further, nor touch thou that man. Quick, go back…'. The monster did as the saint had bidden him and returned to the deep.

LOCH NESS

Inverness

River Ness

Urquhart Castle

Fort Augustus

0   3   6
MILES

From then to the present day there have been thousands of 'sightings' of the monster, some supported by photographic evidence. In 1933 a photograph taken by a London surgeon was published in the London *Daily Mail* . The photograph was taken on the road which runs 60 metres above the loch from a distance of about 180 to 270 metres. It shows what looks like a long, arched neck and thick body in the water.

An American research team set out to investigate the Loch and suspended a

16mm camera, 14 metres below their boat. It took a photograph every 75 seconds and several of them show what is thought to be a red-brown beast with a huge head and arching neck. Sir Peter Scott, the famous naturalist, was convinced by the photographs that a group of prehistoric reptiles had been trapped in the loch at the end of the last Ice Age and had survived.

Does the Loch Ness Monster really exist? (cont.)

The evidence for the existence of the monster, however, is far from conclusive. The photographs are, at best, fuzzy and open to other interpretations. Non-believers claim that the surgeon's photograph could be a mass of rotting vegetation brought to the surface by trapped gases or even the tail of a diving otter photographed to appear bigger than it really is.

Scientific research has often tried to produce evidence of the monster's existence, but has more often than not come away empty handed. In 1961 the Loch Ness Phenomena Investigation Bureau was founded by a member of Parliament called David James. Cameras were set up all around the loch so that it was completely covered but the photographs were disappointingly inconclusive. In 1969, a submersible called *Pisces*, equipped with low-light-level underwater cameras, close-circuit TV and video recording machines was lowered into the loch but no concrete evidence resulted.

In conclusion, while the photographic evidence does not prove that the monster exists, it is equally difficult to prove that what the photographs show is rotting vegetation or diving otters. On the other hand, the use of highly sophisticated technical equipment has not been able to detect this supposedly huge, prehistoric monster in an enclosed and relatively small area of water. It would appear to come down to a question of belief. For those for whom the existence of the monster is a certainty, the lack of scientific evidence is not important. Others, however, are never convinced of anything until they see it with their own eyes.

Formal writing

Learning targets

On completion of this unit the children should be able to:

1 ➤➤ read and understand examples of official language and its characteristic features, e.g. through discussing consumer information, legal documents, layouts, use of footnotes, instructions, parentheses, headings, appendices and asterisks.

2 ➤➤ discuss the way standard English varies in different contexts, e.g. why legal language is necessarily highly formalised, why questionnaires must be specific.

Before you start

Resources for Session 1

Copymaster 45: Rules for Cyclists
Copymaster 46: How does it say this?
Copymaster 47: Say it precisely

Assessment indicators

- Can the children recognise the formal style of 'official' texts as opposed to an informal chatty style?
- Can they appreciate the need for precise language in this context?

Teaching the session

Session 1 ❶ ❷

Introduction 20-30 min

▨ Material which has highly formalised language would, in most cases, be written in contexts with which most children would be unfamiliar. This unit uses the Highway Code which many Year 6 children need to be familiar with for their Cycling Proficiency Test, and concentrates on the precise use of 'official' language.

Give each child **Copymaster 45: Rules for Cyclists** and discuss the following:

- If you were discussing riding a bicycle with a friend would you use language like this?
- Why does it say:

'You should wear a cycle helmet which conforms to current regulations'	rather than	'Have something on your head'
'At night your cycle **MUST** have front and rear lights lit'	rather than	'Put some lights on your bike'
'Use cycle routes where practicable'	rather than	'Always go on cycle lanes'

- Why are **MUST** and **MUST NOT** in capitals and printed in bold?

- Why *should* you do or not do some things whereas you **MUST** or **MUST NOT** do others?

How would the children describe the style of the language used?

Can they say why such language is used?

Why would a chatty, informal style of language not be appropriate?

How does it say this? 20 min

⚫⚫⚫ Give each group **Copymaster 46: How does it say this?** One child in each group can be nominated as the 'scribe' to fill in the copymaster after group discussion.

The phrases they are looking for are:

1 appropriate clothing
2 obscure your lights
3 accessories
4 rear lights
5 where practicable
6 normally located
7 be segregated
8 two abreast
9 affect your balance
10 blind and partially sighted

Summary 10-15 min

Discuss the results of the group discussion with the children. How would they describe the difference between the phrases printed on the copymaster and the phrases they have found from the text? Hopefully they will appreciate that the language of the text is more sophisticated and precise rather than just saying 'it's more difficult'.

Say it precisely 30 min

Copymaster 47: Say it precisely, gives the children a form which people have to fill in to join the local library. It is very unspecific and unhelpful to library staff in its present form.

It would probably be useful to have a discussion with the class about the local library with reference to how the librarians know what type of books to buy and the other services a library provides, e.g.

- Does a librarian only buy books he/she is interested in?
- Why is it useful for a librarian to know the age of the library's borrowers?
- Why is a precise address for each borrower necessary?
- If people wanted to come to the library to study and use reference books what facilities should the library provide? (Chairs and tables.)

The children are required to compose a new form giving the borrower the opportunity to fill in precise details which will be helpful to the library.

They should work in draft form initially for discussion with you. When they think their forms are complete, allow them to word process them for an 'official' presentation. If this is not possible, they should draw lines in the box on the copymaster and copy their form neatly.

Rules for Cyclists

45. Clothing. You should wear
- a cycle helmet which conforms to current regulations
- appropriate clothes for cycling. Avoid clothes which may get tangled in the chain, or in a wheel or may obscure your lights
- light-coloured or fluorescent clothing which helps other road users to see you in daylight and poor light
- reflective clothing and/or accessories (belt, arm or ankle bands) in the dark.

46. At night your cycle **MUST** have front and rear lights lit. It **MUST** also be fitted with a red rear reflector (and amber pedal reflectors, if manufactured after 1/10/85). Flashing lights and other reflectors may help you to be seen but **MUST NOT** be used alone.
Law RVLR regs 18 & 24

When cycling

47. Use cycle routes where practicable. They can make your journey safer.

48. Cycle tracks. These are normally located away from the road, but may occasionally be found alongside footpaths or pavements. Cyclists and pedestrians may be segregated or they may share the same space (unsegregated). When using segregated tracks you **MUST** keep to the side intended for cyclists. Take care when passing pedestrians, especially children, elderly or disabled people, and allow them plenty of room. Always be prepared to slow down and stop if necessary.
Law HA 1835 sect 72

49. Cycle Lanes. These are marked by a white line (which may be broken) along the carriageway. Keep within the lane wherever possible.

50. You **MUST** obey all traffic signs and traffic light signals.
Laws RTA 1988 sect 36, TSRGD reg 10

51. You should
- keep both hands on the handlebars except when signalling or changing gear
- keep both feet on the pedals
- not ride more than two abreast
- ride in single file on narrow or busy roads
- not ride close behind another vehicle
- not carry anything which will affect your balance or may get tangled up with your wheels or chain
- be considerate of other road users, particularly blind and partially sighted pedestrians. Let them know you are there when necessary, for example by ringing your bell.

From *The Highway Code* published by The Department of the Environment, Transport and the Regions. © Crown Copyright 1999

Find the phrases in **Rules for Cyclists** which say:

1 wear sensible clothes _____

2 get in the way of
  your lights _____

3 other things useful
  when you are cycling _____

4 lights at the back of
  your bike _____

5 where it is possible _____

6 usually found _____

7 kept apart _____

8 ride side by side _____

9 make you wobble or
  fall off _____

10 people who can't see _____

Say it precisely

The Grafton Town Library is going to change its membership form. The present one, printed below, does not give them any information about the type of people who want to join the library. It does not tell them:

• the age of the person
• where precisely they live
• what type of books they are interested in
• if they would sometimes borrow videos and/or CDs
• if they would use the reference section for study.

MEMBERSHIP FORM

Name _____

Street _____

Do you read a lot?_____

Compose a new form which will give the library helpful, precise information which they can use when they are buying new books and resources.

MEMBERSHIP FORM

Writing composition
Discursive writing

Choose **one** of the following and write a balanced report which:
- introduces the topic;
- looks at both sides of the argument;
- reaches a conclusion.

In ancient and modern times people have believed in the power of the fortune teller. Are these people really gifted with the ability to see into the future or are they frauds?

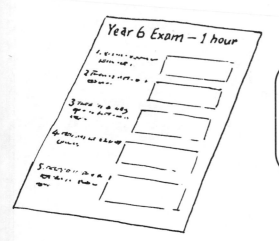

Sometimes quite clever pupils do very badly in exams and tests because they are so nervous. Should exams and tests be abolished?

Some people say that they would find life very difficult without a car, while others say that the car is ruining our world. Should the car be abolished?

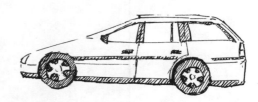

YEAR 6 TERM 3

Focus

Year 6 Term 3 National Literacy non-fiction objectives revise explanatory texts, refine paragraphing skills and require children to review characteristics of non-fiction text type and select appropriate style and form for specific pieces of writing.

As with much of the work at this level, the activities should be viewed as extended pieces of writing which can take place outside of the designated literacy hour.

Content

Unit 1: Explanatory texts
Unit 2: Paragraphs
Unit 3: Purpose and audience

Assessment

Unit 3 provides revision of a wide variety of non-fiction texts which the children have worked with throughout Years 5 and 6. The Copymasters require the children to recall the purpose of each text type and its common features. These Copymasters can be used in class or group work but, if used individually, provide a comprehensive assessment resource for the non-fiction work in the latter half of Key Stage 2.

Curriculum Planner
National Literacy Strategy Planner

This chart shows you how to find activities by unit to resource your term's requirements for text level work on non-fiction. The learning targets closely follow the structure of the non-fiction requirements for the term in the National Literacy Strategy document (page 55). A few of the requirements are not covered.

YEAR 6 Term 3

Range

Non-fiction

- explanations linked to work from other subjects;
- non chronological reports linked to work from other subjects;
- reference texts, a range of dictionaries, thesauruses, including IT sources.

TEXT LEVEL WORK

COMPREHENSION AND COMPOSITION

Reading comprehension

Pupils should be taught:

15 to secure understanding of the features of explanatory texts from Year 5 term 2; Unit 1

19 to review a range of non-fiction text types and their characteristics, discussing when a writer might choose to write in a given style and form; Unit 3

Writing composition

Pupils should be taught:

20 to secure control of impersonal writing, particularly the sustained use of the present tense and the passive voice; Unit 1

21 to divide whole texts into paragraphs, paying attention to the sequence of paragraphs and to the links between one paragraph and the next, e.g. through the choice of appropriate connectives; Unit 2

22 to select the appropriate style and form to suit a specific purpose and audience, drawing on knowledge of different non-fiction text types; Unit 3

UNIT 1 | Explanatory texts

Learning targets

On completion of this unit the children should be able to:

1 ➡ secure understanding of the features of explanatory texts from Year 5 term 2.

2 ➡ secure control of impersonal writing, particularly the sustained use of the present tense and the passive voice.

Before you start

Resources for Session 1

Copymaster 49: Weathering
Copymaster 50: Preparing an explanatory text

Links to other units

Learning Targets for Literacy: Non-Fiction Years 3 and 4 Year 4 Term 2 Unit 3
Learning Targets for Literacy: Non-Fiction Years 5 and 6 Year 5 Term 2 Unit 1

Assessment indicators

- Can the children identify an explanatory text?
- Can they identify and comment on the features of an explanatory text?
- Can they plan, draft and edit an explanatory text using the common features?

Teaching the session

Session 1 ① ②

Introduction [20 min]

Begin the session by recapping on what the children understand by the term 'explanatory text'. Ask for examples of this style of writing and make a list on the board from the children's suggestions.

What can the children remember about the features of explanatory texts?

Revise the following through class discussion:

- impersonal style
  '**A** rabbit's hutch must be kept clean and dry' not '**My/Your** rabbit's hutch…'

- technical language
  Depending on what the explanatory text is about, the children should use the correct vocabulary:
  'Wild rabbits live underground in **warrens**' not 'Wild rabbits live underground in **holes**'.

- passive voice
  It is not necessary to write an entire explanatory text in the passive voice, but it should include several examples of this form of sentence construction:
  '**Fresh food is needed by rabbits** if they are to remain healthy' not '**Rabbits need fresh food** if they are to remain healthy'.

- present tense:
  'Rabbits **are** often kept as pets' not 'Rabbits **were** kept as pets'

- linking words and phrases
  These are used to help the reader move sequentially through the explanation, signalling 'the next stage':
  'At this stage', 'During this time', 'After this', 'As a result', etc. **Not** 'And then', 'Then', etc.

If appropriate, look back at **Copymasters 9 and 10** to refresh the children's memories of explanatory texts they have worked on.

Analysing an explanatory text [20 min]

Copymaster 49: Weathering, gives the children another opportunity to analyse an explanatory text. **Copymaster 11** can be used for the children to make notes on in preparation for a class discussion.

Summary [10 min]

The children can compare their findings through class discussion. Investigate the usefulness of labelled diagrams for this piece of text. Do the children think the text is sufficient in itself or would diagrams be helpful? What other forms of illustration might be useful? (e.g photographs)

Writing an explanatory text   30 min

 This activity can bring together a variety of skills which the children have learned throughout this book and should be viewed as an extended writing activity that can take place outside of the literacy hour.

Begin by suggesting topics on which the children can write an explanatory text, linked to work in other curriculum areas if possible. They should then follow a process of:

Research

- their own general knowledge;
- use of the class/school library;
- CD-ROMs and other software.

Note-making

- writing relevant information in note form;
- compiling a bibliography.

Drafting

- organising their notes into paragraphs;
- making an initial draft from their notes;
- sketch out illustrations.

Editing

- to ensure spelling and grammar are correct;
- to ensure the style of the draft includes the required common features of impersonal style, passive voice, present tense, technical language and linking words and phrases.

Final draft

- make a neat copy of the work with suitable title;
- include detailed illustrations, i.e. annotated or labelled diagrams;
- word process if possible.

The stages of this process are repeated on **Copymaster 50: Preparing an explanatory text**, for the children to use as a check list. Be on hand to guide the children through the various stages, especially during:

- note-making: remind them of the 'key word' approach and not to slavishly copy every word;
- editing: have they explained each stage clearly? Have they checked spelling, especially of technical terms?

Weathering

Weathering is the break up of rock caused by exposure to the weather; in particular rain, heat and cold. Weathering breaks up and weakens the surface of the rock, allowing erosion to take place which wears away and removes the loosened material.

Freeze-thaw weathering is caused by water seeping into cracks in rocks, road surfaces and buildings and then freezing. As the water freezes it expands, and pressure is exerted on the sides of the crack causing them to break up.

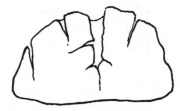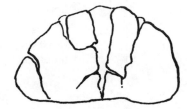

Another form of weathering is called biological weathering. This is caused by plants and animals. Plants or tree roots may grow in cracks in rocks, gradually forcing them apart. Burrowing animals, such as rabbits and moles, can also aid the weathering process by removing soil which then allows water to reach the rocks below.

A third type of weathering is called onion weathering. This happens when rocks are repeatedly heated and cooled. Heat causes the outer layer of rock to expand slightly and then as it cools, it contracts. Continual expansion and contraction cause small pieces of rock to break off like the skin of an onion. This type of weathering is common in desert areas, where the daytime temperature can reach 70°C and the night-time temperature can fall below freezing.

A further type of weathering is known as chemical weathering which is caused by acidic water. Ordinary rainwater contains a small amount of acid. The rocks are attacked and eaten away by the acid. The rate of chemical weathering increases in warm, moist conditions.

50 | Preparing an explanatory text

Research

- own general knowledge ☐
- use of the class/school library ☐
- CD-ROMs and other software ☐

Note-making

- write relevant information in note form ☐
- compile a bibliography ☐

Drafting

- organise notes into paragraphs ☐
- make an initial draft from notes ☐
- sketch out illustrations ☐

Editing

- ensure spelling and grammar are correct ☐
- ensure the style of the draft includes the required common features:

  - impersonal style ☐
  - passive voice ☐
  - present tense ☐
  - technical language ☐
  - linking words and phrases ☐

Final draft

- make a neat copy of the work with suitable title ☐
- include detailed illustrations, i.e. annotated/labelled diagrams ☐
- word process if possible ☐

UNIT 2 Paragraphs

Learning target

On completion of this unit the children should be able to:

1 ➤➤ divide whole texts into paragraphs, paying attention to the sequence of paragraphs and to the links between one paragraph and the next, e.g. through the choice of appropriate connectives.

Before you start

Resources for Session 1

Copymaster 51: Why paragraph?
Copymaster 52: Organising notes into paragraphs

Links to other units

Learning Targets for Literacy: Non-Fiction Years 3 and 4 Year 4 Term 2 Unit 2

Assessment indicators

- Can the children identify the reasons for paragraphing?
- Can they research and organise notes from different sources into a paragraph plan?

Teaching the session

Session 1   ①

Introduction   20 min

▦ Paragraphing has been an integral part of the organisation of the text types the children have investigated throughout this book, but it is useful to spend a session looking at the reasons for using paragraphs, and the link between the note-making process and paragraphing.

Begin by asking the children what they understand by the term 'paragraph' and how they would use them in their own written work.

Give each child **Copymaster 51: Why paragraph?** which gives examples of paragraphed text for analysis.

1 Hong Kong

This is an introductory and second paragraph. Discuss:

- the purpose of an introductory paragraph;
- why a second paragraph has been started;
- the link between the two paragraphs;
- would the writing be improved or not improved by changing the order of the paragraphs?

2 Water pollution

These are two paragraphs from the body of a report on water pollution. Discuss:

- why two paragraphs are needed;
- the link between the two paragraphs;
- the opening words in each paragraph;
- would the writing be improved or not improved by changing the order of the paragraphs?

3 Acid rain

These are three paragraphs from the body of an explanatory text. Discuss:

- why three paragraphs are needed;
- the link between the paragraphs;
- the linking words and phrases;
- would the writing be improved or not improved by changing the order of the paragraphs?

Through discussion you should conclude that:

- an introductory paragraph 'sets the scene' for the reader, i.e. introduces the topic to be written about in general terms and should always come first;
- a new paragraph should be used for a different aspect or part of the topic;
- a new paragraph should be used for each stage of a process in an explanatory text.

Organising notes into paragraphs   20-25 min

♣ Give each group **Copymaster 52: Organising notes into paragraphs**. The copymaster shows notes made from three different information sources about Disney World. The children are required to group the notes in such a way that information for different paragraphs is assembled. They can do this by numbering the information, e.g.

1. introductory paragraph
2. second paragraph

or by using different coloured highlighters. It is helpful to write headings and put the information in the relevant list.

Summary 15-20min

Discuss the ordering of the notes with the children, writing their suggestions on the board. One way of ordering the notes into paragraphs is as follows:

Introductory paragraph

*   central Florida – Orlando
*   most popular man-made tourist attraction on Earth
*   opened 1971
*   as big as San Francisco

Second paragraph

main theme parks:

*   Magic Kingdom – see Mickey Mouse, Donald Duck, 3 o'clock parade, Jungle Cruise, Adventureland, Frontierland
*   Epcot Centre – opened Oct 1982 – shows new ideas + technologies from all over the world. Most popular ride – Spaceship Earth
*   MGM Studios

Third paragraph

water parks:

*   Typhoon Lagoon – is largest, water slides, rapids, exotic fish
*   River Country – rope swings, rocky mountain landscape

Fourth paragraph

other attractions:

*   Busch Gardens – 300 acre theme park, 1 hour drive from Orlando
*   Kennedy Space Centre – east coast, Apollo launch pads, Space Museum

*   Sea World – killer whale called Shamu, 'Terrors of the Deep' – sharks

Fifth paragraph

Accommodation – hotels in all theme parks and in Orlando

Go on to discuss:

*   should any of the paragraphs be further divided into more paragraphs? For example one paragraph for each park in 'main theme parks'.
*   do any areas need more research? (e.g. MGM Studios.)
*   can any of the information be left out? (Possibly the fifth paragraph.)

Using paragraphs 30min

This activity is best left to your discretion so the children can research, make and order notes and write up in paragraphs a subject which is relevant to current topic work. As with other work at this level, it can be viewed as an extended writing activity and take place outside of the designated literacy hour.

Alternatively, you can give the children a country or city to research asking them to make notes on:

*   its location;
*   main features, e.g. mountains, rivers, etc.;
*   climate;
*   what tourists might go to see;
*   agriculture;
*   industry.

The children should make notes from books and IT sources, order their notes under headings as a paragraph plan and write a first draft for you to check before making a neat copy. At the draft stage discuss with each child why they have begun new paragraphs where they have, to ascertain if they have grasped the concept.

51 Why Paragraph?

1

Most Hong Kong festivals celebrate the birth of a god or legendary hero. They are dazzling and noisy events, with streets full of happy people.

Chinese new year is a very important festival in Hong Kong. It begins between late January and mid-February and lasts for 15 days.

2

In urban areas water is polluted by factories discharging chemicals into rivers. Waste materials such as lead and copper are discharged from factories every day. Water treatment plants also produce pollutants such as chlorine and copper, and oil refineries discharge polluted water.

In rural areas, groundwater and rivers are polluted by farm slurry or liquid manure, fertilisers and pesticides.

3

Power stations emit pollutants. Some fall to the ground whereas others are taken up into the sky by the movement of the air.

At this stage the pollutants then mix with the water vapour in the clouds forming a weak acid such as sulphuric acid or nitric acid.

Finally, the rain falls from these polluted clouds as acid rain.

Organising notes into paragraphs

52

Guide to Disney World

central Florida

most popular man-made tourist attraction on Earth

theme parks: Epcot Centre – opened October 1982 – shows new ideas and technologies from all over the world

Magic Kingdom: Mickey Mouse – Donald Duck – 3 o'clock parade

water parks: Typhoon Lagoon – largest water park – water slides/rapids/exotic fish

hundreds of hotels

other attractions – Sea World

Find Out About Disney World

main theme park: Magic Kingdom – has Jungle Cruise/ Adventure Land/Frontierland

other attractions: Busch Gardens – 300 acre theme park about an hour's drive

River Country: water park – rope swings/rocky mountain landscape

Disney World opened 1971 Epcot Centre – theme park – most popular ride: Spaceship Earth

A Holiday of a Lifetime

main theme parks: Magic Kingdom
                    Epcot Centre
                    MGM Studios

other attractions outside Disney World:
Sea world – killer whale called Shamu, 'Terrors of the Deep' – sharks
Kennedy Space Centre – east coast – see Apollo launch pads and Space Museum
accommodation: hotels in each of the theme parks
plenty of hotels in Orlando itself
Disney World in Orlando, Florida. As big as San Francisco

Purpose and audience

Learning targets

On completion of this unit the children should be able to:

1 ➤ review a range of non-fiction text types and their characteristics, discussing when a writer might choose to write in a given style and form.

2 ➤ select the appropriate style and form to suit a specific purpose and audience, drawing on knowledge of different non-fiction text types.

Before you start

Resources

Copymaster 53: Report writing
Copymaster 54: Instructions
Copymaster 55: Explanatory texts
Copymaster 56: Formal letters

Copymaster 57: Editorials
Copymaster 58: Advertising
Copymaster 59: Journalistic writing
Copymaster 60: Non-chronological reports
Copymaster 61: Discursive texts

Teaching the sessions

Introduction

This final unit has a different format to previous units. To fulfil the NLS objectives the children must revisit the non-fiction texts they have worked on throughout Years 5 and 6.

This unit can be used for the overall assessment of the non-fiction work done in the second half of Key Stage 2. It is recommended that the activities are spread out over a number of sessions.

What this unit provides is a series of copymasters with:

• the opening extract of a particular style of non-fiction writing which the children have worked on. The extract is given to 'jog' the children's memory as to the style of non-fiction text they are looking at. The Copymaster where the full text appears can be used as a reference if required.

• an 'analysis' box where the children can note:

    the purpose of the writing

    things to think about, e.g. common features, audience, etc.

• a choice of writing activities relevant to the style.

Below is a summary of the important features and the purpose of each type of non-fiction text the children are required to analyse.

Copymaster 53: Report writing

Purpose: to inform

Things to think about: opening paragraph to orientate reader
     logical paragraph sequence
     audience
     usually past tense

Reading Copymaster: 1

Writing Copymaster: 2

Copymaster 54: Instructions

Purpose: to enable reader to do or make something

Things to think about: listing equipment
     logical, detailed sequence
     numbered points
     short, easily understood sentences
     imperative verbs

Reading Copymaster: 3

Writing Copymaster: 4

Copymaster 55: Explanatory texts

Purpose: to explain how something happens/a process

Things to think about: opening paragraph to
      orientate reader
      logical sequence of
      paragraphs
      link words and phrases
      impersonal style
      technical language
      passive voice
      present tense

Reading Copymaster: 9 and 10

Writing Copymaster: 12

Copymaster 56: Formal letters

Purpose: to inform, persuade, protest or complain

Things to think about: address of sender
      address of recipient
      opening paragraph to explain
      the purpose of the letter
      formal style and vocabulary,
      not 'chatty'
      correct ending to match
      opening

Reading Copymaster: 16, 17, 20 and 21

Writing Copymaster: 19 and 23

Copymaster 57: Editorials

Purpose: to put forward one point of view in a persuasive style

Things to think about: an issue of local/national
      interest
      fact and opinion
      persuasive words and phrases
      conclusion supporting one
      point of view

Reading Copymaster: 24 and 25

Writing Copymaster: 26

Copymaster 58: Advertising

Purpose: to persuade

Things to think about: language of persuasion
      audience appeal
      word play
      layout
      visual impact

Reading Copymaster: 27

Writing Copymaster: 28

Copymaster 59: Journalistic writing

Purpose: to inform, entertain or persuade

Things to think about: facts
      bias
      balanced reporting
      how writer interprets facts
      headline

Reading Copymaster: 36 and 37

Writing Copymaster: 38

Copymaster 60: Non-chronological reports

Purpose: to inform

Things to think about: research
      note-making
      opening paragraph to
      orientate reader
      grouping facts in paragraph
      structure
      mostly present tense
      acknowledging sources
      bibliography

Reading Copymaster: 39

Writing Copymaster: 40

Copymaster 61: Discursive texts

Purpose: to present conflicting points of view and reach a conclusion

Things to think about: opening paragraph to
      introduce topic under
      discussion
      present supporting points of
      view
      present points of view which
      refute, summarise and
      conclude

Reading Copymaster: 44

Writing Copymaster: 43

53

Report writing

The report

A visit to Ordsall Hall

This term our class has been studying the Tudors. On the 23rd of April we went on a trip to Ordsall Hall, which is a Tudor house in Salford near Manchester.

We left school at 9.30a.m. and arrived at Ordsall Hall at 10.30a.m. We had sketch books and notebooks with us so that we could draw and make notes on the Tudor objects in the house and the decoration on the building.

Our tour of the house began in the Great Hall . . .

Style

Purpose: _____

_____

Things to think about: _____

_____

_____

_____

_____

_____

Writing activities

Write a report on one of the following.

[a local event]   [a school event]   [taking part in a sporting activity]

How not to write instructions!

Sort it out!

I have used 'Learn To Spell' on the computer and I have to write instructions so that other people in the class can use it as well.

   'Learn To Spell' is a CD-ROM which you have to put into the computer. Don't put it in the slit for the floppy discs. You have to put it in the CD-ROM tray which slides out when you press the button. You have to turn on the computer first. The switch for turning on the computer…

Style

Purpose: _____

_____

Things to think about: _____

_____

_____

_____

_____

Writing activities

Write instructions for one of the following activities.

| cleaning your shoes | playing a computer game | making a paper aeroplane |

Explanatory texts

Explanation

The digestive system

Digestion means the breaking down of food so that the body can absorb and use it. Food is broken down in two stages:

The first stage is when the food is chewed in the mouth. This part of the digestive process is quite quick.

The second stage takes much longer and begins when the food passes down the gullet from the mouth.

The food first enters the stomach and mixes with enzymes…

Style

Purpose: _____

_____

Things to think about: _____

_____

_____

_____

_____

_____

Writing activities

Write an explanation for one of the following.

the water cycle

a food chain

how a bulb lights up in a circuit

Formal letters

A letter of complaint

> 5, Beech Lane
> Slugsville
> Lancashire
> 17th December
>
> Slugsville Council
> The Town Hall
> Slugsville
>
> Dear Sir or Madam,
>   I live in a small cottage in Beech Lane, a narrow cul-de-sac on the edge of the town.
>   As you are no doubt aware, over the past few days there have been heavy snowfalls and, as a consequence, Beech Lane has been totally blocked. I have been unable to get my car down the lane and, with the infrequent bus service in my part of town, getting to work has proved very difficult.
>   Snow ploughs and gritting lorries have been at work in other parts of the town...

Style

Purpose: _____

_____

Things to think about: _____

_____

_____

_____

_____

_____

Writing activities

Choose one of the following and write a formal letter:

to complain about rubbish collection in your street.	to inform the road dept. that a large hole has appeared in the road in front of your house.	to persuade the local shop to provide a litter bin outside the shop.

The *Howden Herald* Editorial

Is it time to stop making our town centres into ghost towns?

Our front page reports on the proposed building of a supermarket on the north-east edge of our town.

Surely it is time that local planners saw sense? Every time a supermarket or retail park is built near a town the shops in the town centre suffer. Every right-thinking person can see this.

Many of the shopkeepers along the High Street have been there for years, providing the people of Howden with a service which we seem to take for granted. Shopkeepers are voters too…

Style

Purpose: _____

_____

Things to think about: _____

_____

_____

_____

_____

_____

Writing activities

Write an editorial about one of the following.

| plans to knock down the local library to make way for a car park | plans to raise the admission prices at the swimming baths | an issue of your choice |

Would this persuade you to buy?

> THE ONLY CAR TO BE SEEN IN!

> Give your kids the best start to the day.

> You won't find a lower price!

> The professionals' choice

Style

Purpose: _____

_____

Things to think about: _____

_____

_____

_____

_____

_____

Writing activities

Write an advertisement for one of the following.

| a toothpaste | a computer game | a chocolate bar |

Biased or balanced?

The Town Crier

25p   Saturday 21st February

Better Team Beaten

Stanton Wanderers 0   Biggin United 1

by Alex Boots

Saturday's football match at Stanton's ground saw the better side beaten by a fluke goal in the 77th minute.

Up until that luckiest of goals, Stanton Wanderers were by far the better side. They had the ball most of the time, hardly allowing Biggin United into the game.

Stanton's midfield players passed superbly, especially Ian Wrong who controlled the match from his position as centre forward.

Carter and Maine, Stanton's defenders…

Style

Purpose: _____

_____

Things to think about: _____

_____

_____

_____

_____

_____

Writing activities

Write a balanced newspaper report about one of the following.

two neighbours arguing about mending the fence which divides their properties

a sporting event of your choice

Find the facts about Italy

situated in southern Europe

main rivers – Po, Tiber, Arno, Adige

275 BC most of country ruled from Rome

(*A short history of Italy*, M. Frome)

two main offshore islands – Sicily/Sardinia

main crops – wheat/maize

after 4th century AD invaded by barbarian tribes,
e.g. Visigoths/Vandals

principal manufactured goods – textiles/chemicals

(*Worldwide Encyclopaedia*)

Style

Purpose: _____

_____

Things to think about: _____

_____

_____

_____

_____

_____

Writing activities

Write a non-chronological report about one of the following.

| a place you have visited on holiday | a specific animal kept as a pet | your hobby |

Let's look at the evidence

Does the Loch Ness Monster really exist?

The Loch Ness Monster is a subject which has fascinated people from the first supposed sighting in AD 565 to the present day. Many people are convinced the monster exists in the deep water of the Scottish loch, while others are equally sure that it is just a figment of the imagination.

The first sighting of the Loch Ness Monster was some 1400 years ago by St Columba. One of St Columba's followers was swimming across the loch to fetch a boat when, suddenly, the monster appeared at the surface…

Style

Purpose: _____

_____

Things to think about: _____

_____

_____

_____

_____

_____

Writing activities

Write discursively about one of the following.

smoking should be banned in all public places	people should be made to retire at 50	all young people should stay in full-time education until they are 18